Herb
gardening
— *For* —
beginners

DEREK FELL

Herb
gardening
—— For ——
beginners

DEREK FELL

FRIEDMAN/FAIRFAX
PUBLISHERS

A FRIEDMAN/FAIRFAX BOOK

Please visit our website: www.metrobooks.com

Library of Congress Cataloging-in-Publication Data available upon request.

ISBN 1-58663-020-2

Editor: Susan Lauzau
Art Director: Jeff Batzli
Designers: Susan E. Livingston and John Gaines
Photography Director: Christopher C. Bain

Color separations by Bright Arts Graphics (S) Pte Ltd.
Printed in the United Kingdom by Butler & Tanner Ltd.

1 3 5 7 9 10 8 6 4 2

Distributed by Sterling Publishing Company, Inc.
387 Park Avenue South
New York, NY 10016
Distributed in Canada by Sterling Publishing
Canadian Manda Group
One Atlantic Avenue, Suite 105
Toronto, Ontario, Canada M6K 3E7
Distributed in Australia by
Capricorn Link (Australia) Pty, Ltd.
P.O. Box 704, Windsor, NSW 2756 Australia

Frontispiece: A spectacular planting of lavender, thyme, dill, and other herbs makes this driveway border something special.

Dedication

For my three children, Christina, Victoria, and Derek Jr.,
all of whom love gardening.

Acknowledgments

In recent years I have enjoyed creating a series of twenty-two theme gardens at my home, Cedaridge Farm, in Bucks County, Pennsylvania, including several herb gardens. Most of what we grow is for culinary use and for my wife, Carolyn, to make fragrant dried arrangements. Indeed, Thanksgiving to Christmas at Cedaridge Farm is like a fifth season—one of the most colorful times of the year, thanks to her creative energy in decorating every room of the house, and all of the outbuildings.

The success of our herb plantings, however, would not be possible without the help of my grounds supervisor, Wendy Fields, who ensures that the herb gardens are always picture perfect.

Also, my sincere thanks to Kathy Nelson, my office manager, who helps keep my extensive photo library organized. Through her dedication to detail we maintain accurate records of everything that grows at Cedaridge Farm.

Finally, a heartfelt thanks to Louise and Cyrus Hyde, owners of Well-Sweep Herb Farm of Port Murray, New Jersey, for allowing me the freedom to photograph their spectacular herb garden.

Contents

Opposite: Herbs, like these purple-headed chives, combine well with vegetables in a kitchen garden.

Introduction

Enthusiasm for growing and using herbs is at an all-time high—and no wonder! Herbs have become popular for both their ornamental qualities and for their exceptional usefulness. Not only do herbs add wonderful flavors to foods, but many also have proven medicinal value. The burgeoning field of aromatherapy uses uplifting herbal fragrances in facial massages, luxurious herbal baths, and inhalations to relieve stress. Herbs are even thought to reduce the risk of certain cancers, and psychiatrists are using them to explore memory loss treatments.

Another benefit to growing herbs: a few plants go a long way. Many beautiful herb gardens have been designed in small spaces, and even the tiniest plot will allow you to grow a varied sampling of herbs that will enhance both your dinners and the look of your garden.

My interest in herbs began when I was just a child; I spent many happy hours watching my father prepare a special savory stuffing for the Christmas goose or turkey using aromatic herbs with magical names like rosemary, tarragon, and thyme. When I moved to the United States from England, I became hooked on vegetable gardening; harvests of homegrown vegetables and an interest in cooking with the freshest of foods prompted me to begin growing culinary herbs, which I used to flavor gallons of soup and other dishes.

This fascination with herbs grew when I traveled to France, where I was stunned by the beauty of a lavender farm in Provence. It was mid-July and there had been little rain for several weeks, yet the lavender was in full flower, stretching out like a blue haze for acres. A dirt track curved through an avenue of olive trees up to a cozy pantile-roofed stone farmhouse. I befriended the farmer and he allowed me to photograph there for two days. My bedroom overlooked his potager and the fragrant fields of lavender beyond. When I told him that this farm was my idea of paradise, he urged me to hike a steep gravel trail to a nearby ruined castle, Chateauneuf. There, I marveled at the sweeps of fragrant wild lavender that clothed the mountain slopes as far as I could see! Immediately, I resolved to plant a small lavender garden at my home, Cedaridge Farm, to remind me of that memorable day.

As a garden photographer, I am always thrilled to discover imaginative herb garden designs—both formal and informal—tucked away in odd corners of some country garden, historical property, or large estate. For years I would drive north to Port Murray, New Jersey, and marvel at the work of the Hydes, a husband-and-wife team who run a busy herb business from Well Sweep Herb Farm, near the Delaware Water Gap. On my first visit I remember Cyrus Hyde throwing open the huge double doors of a windowless barn to reveal inside what looked like an Aladdin's cave of treasure: every inch of space from ceiling to floor was filled with the jewellike colors of drying herbs and wreaths. The aroma, of course, was unbelievable. I stood transfixed for several minutes, deeply inhaling the mixture of sweet fragrances, and resolved someday to have my own barn for drying herbs.

There are several great reasons to start an herb garden of your own. First and foremost is that herbs are relatively easy to grow. Many come from the driest parts of the Mediterranean and North Africa, where they have learned to survive in a harsh environment. Then there is the added benefit of *usefulness*. In addition to providing great flavorings, herbs can be a source of insect repellents (see page 61) and natural dyes (see pages 42–43).

Some of the therapeutic and medicinal values of herbs are backed by solid research. The gel inside aloe vera leaves, for example, is good for the relief of burns, while the fragrance of mints and eucalyptus leaves can clear blocked sinuses. Other easy-to-grow herbs are effective as air fresheners and deodorizers. Sweet Annie and rose-scented geraniums make great household deodorizers, freshening any room in the house.

Herbs have long been brewed into refreshing teas, and herbal teas continue to be popular. Chamomile and lavender teas soothe the senses, while other herbs, including basil and rosemary, act as stimulants, providing an energy boost and reducing mental fatigue. Ginseng tea is even reputed to act as an aphrodisiac, though this is unproven.

But perhaps the most intriguing use for herbs is their value in garden design. Herbs offer a more subtle charm in the landscape than most annuals and perennials, and they require a more sophisticated approach to design. But a fabulous herb garden invariably leaves more of an impression on visitors than the best annual or perennial gardens, since herbs add touchable textures and inviting scents as well as visual pleasure.

Of course, the terms annual and perennial could technically be

When visitors walk the flagstone path to this bench, their footsteps release the pleasant aroma of creeping thyme, which is planted between the stones.

used to describe the majority of plants used in herb gardens—annuals completing their life cycles in a single season and perennials living on for several generations. However, there are also herbs classified as bulbs (chives, for example), which live on from year to year; biennials like parsley, which complete their life cycles in 2 years; and woody plants, such as bay, which develop a durable cell structure that has a longer life expectancy than any of these.

Though the Bible refers to any green growing plant (including trees) as an herb, and there seems to be no clear-cut horticultural definition, we tend to think of herbs as any useful garden plant that can't be classified as a vegetable or an ornamental. The term *herb* has no botanical recognition, but it is generally used to describe plants with parts that can be used fresh for culinary or medicinal purposes. Nor is there a clear-cut distinction between an herb and a spice. In the seed trade, the term herb is generally used to define useful annual or perennial plants that are propagated by seeds or

Above: A corner of the spice market in Fez, Morocco, offers a vast array of dried herbs and spices. Right: Herb products line the shelves of the flower market in Nice.

cuttings, while spices are regarded as the dried or powdered aromatic product of mostly woody plants, such as cinnamon and cloves. But in the spice market in Fez, Morocco, the most incredible fresh food market I have ever seen, powdered mint was referred to as a spice and fresh mint was described as an herb.

There is also a fine line between the accepted notion of a culinary vegetable and an herb. We tend to regard vegetables such as potatoes and lettuce as important food crops, while herbs are used mostly as seasonings. Yet certain plants can be classified as both a vegetable and an herb: celery, for example, is not only a valuable food crop; its seeds are aromatic and useful in flavoring.

Juniper trunks form a raised bed for a collection of basil varieties, including cinnamon basil and green curled basil.

The cultivation of herbs is nearly as old as civilization itself. During the Renaissance, herbs and spices were valued so highly that traveling merchants opened up "spice routes" to move more of this precious commodity, and voyages of exploration were financed to find the shortest routes. Indeed, when the Emperor Charlemagne issued the Capitulare de Villis decree, a mandate aimed at organizing his subjects into making the most fruitful use of their land, eighty-nine herbs for seasonings and healing were on the list. It was the prospect of finding new routes to India and China, both of which offered valuable trade opportunities for spices, that launched Christopher Columbus on the transatlantic voyage that resulted in the discovery of the Americas. Ironically, his discovery of North America yielded many wonderful new vegetables (such as potatoes, peppers, pumpkins, and corn), but very few new herbs or spices.

With the advent of synthetic substitutes for many of the natural flavorings, perfumes, and medicines—and the handy packaging of dried herbs and spices—the herb garden lost its place as a necessity of life. But today herb gardens are enjoying a strong revival: people are discovering that fresh, organically grown herbs are infinitely better than those commercially grown and dried.

The revival of herb gardens is also a matter of a rekindling of romance: the lure of uplifting fragrances and the hint of exoticism, as well as a renewed appreciation of more subtle foliage and flowers, all play a part in the herbal renaissance. The long and storied history of herbs and the sense of communion with nature they provide are also part of the attraction that has made herb gardening a premier pastime.

This book shows not only how to use herbs in creative garden designs, but also how to grow and propagate them, how to employ them effectively around the home, and how to choose the most useful herbs for modern gardens.

Derek Fell
Cedaridge Farm
Gardenville, Pennsylvania

Victoria Fell gathers herbs for potpourri

in the garden at Cedaridge Farm.

Planning
and
Planting

Opposite: This combination herb and cutting garden at the Stanford Inn in Mendocino, California, is laid out with wide paths of grass so that all the plants are easy to reach for harvesting.

Site and Soil Requirements

Raised beds make working the soil and harvesting herbs much easier. Here, 'Repens' winter savory planted at the corner of the bed creates a dome of attractive white flowers.

Most herbs demand a well-drained soil in a sunny location. Some, like watercress and horseradish, will grow with their roots permanently covered with water, but even these exceptions will also grow well in regular garden soil. So if you're interested in an herb garden, it is better to err on the side of a sandy, dry soil rather than a heavy, wet one.

Whatever your soil, make sure that the site gets at least 6 hours of sun each day. To measure the amount of sunlight a specific site receives, stake out your proposed plot with string and time the number of hours the area is completely filled with sun. If the shadow of a tree limb crosses the string into the plot before 6 hours are up, consider removing the offending limbs to admit more light; sometimes the removal of a single tree limb can add enough light to turn a too-shady site into a usable garden site.

To check whether your proposed site has adequate drainage, dig a hole 1 foot (30cm) wide and 2 feet (60cm) deep in the center of your site, and pour water into the hole until it is filled. Then measure the amount of time it takes for the hole to drain. If most of the water is gone after an hour, the site has good drainage; if the hole is still full after 3 hours, the drainage is poor. There are several ways to improve drainage. First, consider creating a raised bed. Using stones, landscape ties, or bricks, raise the soil level at least 12 inches (30cm) above the surrounding soil surface. To improve drainage even more, you may need to dig a ditch and lay a drainage pipe from the site to a catchment that can take away excess water.

Most soils fall between two extremes: clay and sand. Clay soil is made up of tiny soil particles that bind together into a solid, heavy, impervious mass. Scoop some up in your hand and squeeze it; the soil will compact into a smooth, squishy lump. Plant roots find it extremely difficult to penetrate clay soils in their search for nutrients. The remedy is to dig down to a depth of at least 12 inches (30cm) and add plenty of humus.

Brightening the Shade

In general, herbs prefer a sunny, rather than a shady, location, except in warm climates, where some shade helps to provide a respite from the stress of heat and humidity. Few herbs will survive a deeply shaded location—for example, a site that is overhung with dense evergreens, a setting permanently shaded by a dark, high wall, or one that is shaded by a combination of a wall and tree.

You can brighten a shady location by painting the surrounding surfaces white and, of course, trimming tree branches. One of the most successful herbs for a shady situation is sweet woodruff (shown here growing beneath azalea bushes), which will create a beautiful, fragrant, weed-suffocating ground cover. Ginseng is another herb that does well in the deep shade, although you must provide it with a fertile, humus-rich soil and regular watering during dry spells.

The best sources of humus are peat (available in bales from garden centers), well-decomposed animal manure, leaf mold, and garden compost. If the clay is particularly heavy, add gypsum, which is also available from garden centers. Both humus and gypsum provide the aeration

To create a new bed for herbs, remove the turf and dig down into the soil to a depth of one spade. Place the soil on a tarp or burlap sack and reserve it for conditioning. Next, dig down a second spade's depth and deposit that soil on a second tarp.

necessary to improve heavy, clay soil. Avoid adding only sand, which, without humus, will create a soil with the consistency of peanut butter.

Sand and gravel (both composed of large soil particles) are not bad growing mediums for most herbs, since drainage tends to be excellent and plant roots can penetrate freely. But sand and gravel have poor anchorage and moisture-holding capacity. Nutrients also leach from the soil too quickly. To improve a sandy or gravelly soil, the answer is again to add lots of humus. To improve 12 inches (30cm) of sand, you may need to add as much as 6 inches (15cm) of good humus. In local gravelly soil it's also a good idea to add some screened garden topsoil, carted in from a local farm, garden center, or nursery.

In addition to the consistency of the soil, herbs are affected by soil chemistry, particularly its pH factor. Soil pH is a measure of acidity or alkalinity. Highly acidic soils generally occur in forested areas with high rainfall, while alkaline soils exist in desert areas or where glaciers have scraped away the topsoil to reveal limestone deposits. The ideal growing medium for the majority of herbs is a neutral soil. To find out if you have a pH imbalance you will need to conduct a soil test.

There are inexpensive do-it-yourself pH kits on the market, but they are usually imprecise and don't adequately tell you how to correct your soil imbalance. It is far better to have your soil tested by a soil laboratory; any garden center will provide you with a name and address for a lab.

The soil lab will supply a bag to place soil samples in and some forms to fill out stating what types of plants you wish to grow. After you mail the sample to the soil laboratory, you will receive a detailed computer printout that tells you not only the pH of your soil, but also any nutrient deficiencies your soil might have. More importantly, the printout will explain precisely how to correct your pH imbalance (usually by adding sulphur for an overly alkaline soil or lime for an overly acidic soil), and how to correct any nutrient imbalance (usually by adding a granular fertilizer). Most soil tests will also tell you whether your soil needs a conditioner, such as humus.

For the most part, herbs are not heavy feeders, and fertilizing is usually not as important as it is for fruit or vegetable gardens. Garden compost, raked into the upper soil surface in the spring, is generally all the feeding your herbs will need.

Preparing a New Bed

This newly dug bed shows the soil from both levels, on either side of the plot. After being improved with humus and fertilizer, the soil will be replaced in the bed.

When you start from scratch to prepare a special bed for herbs, consider the advantages of double digging the soil in the plot. This is a simple process that will ensure that you have an excellent growing medium for your herbs, and is indeed a good way to begin any garden bed. First, remove any surface grass with a flat-ended spade so that the bare soil is exposed. Once the entire area of the plot has been freed of grass, dig down to the depth of the spade, piling the soil onto a tarp beside the plot. Next,

dig down another spade depth and place that soil onto a separate tarp. Remove any stones, weed roots, grubs, and debris that you find in the soil. Mix compost or peat moss, plus a granular fertilizer, into the soil on the tarps. If your soil's pH has been tested and found to need adjustment, add either lime (for a soil that is too acidic) or sulphur (for a soil that is too alkaline). Then replace the soil, shoveling the topsoil in first, then placing the subsoil on top.

This practice of double digging will fluff up the soil and provide ideal conditions for growing a wide range of healthy herbs. Usually, the practice of double digging and adding soil conditioner like compost will raise the soil several inches above the original soil level, so consider edging the bed with stones, brick, or logs to retain it, especially if the site slopes.

Planting

When planting container-grown herbs, be sure to dig a hole deep enough to accommodate all the roots. Here, a trowel creates a hole between flagstones big enough for the transplanted thyme.

Though many herbs—such as chervil, dill, and coriander—can be seeded directly into the garden, others, such as lavender, may have erratic germination. Still others, like bay, simply grow too slowly from seed. These are good candidates to purchase as transplants from a nursery or garden center. When choosing herbs to transplant, avoid those that look top-heavy; instead, select compact, healthy-looking specimens, 3 to 4 inches (7.5 to 10 cm) tall.

Slide the herb plants out of their pots, trying not to disturb the roots. If the roots are matted and tangled, gently tease them away from the bottom and sides of the container, allowing them freedom to grow out into the soil. With a trowel, make a hole large enough to easily accommodate the transplant, set the herb plant in the hole, and firm the soil around the roots. Leave a slight depression in the soil around the main stem to serve as a water catchment. Water the transplant immediately, and keep the surrounding soil free of weeds.

Tender herbs like basil should be hardened-off in a cold frame before they are transplanted in the garden.

In general, herbs are drought-tolerant and susceptible to rot if overwatered. They generally require watering only when the soil surface feels dry. Herbs are also efficient at extracting nutrients from even impoverished soils, but a mild liquid fertilizer applied to the foliage and root zone at the time of planting will ensure that your transplants get off to a good start.

Many herbs are hardy, and will tolerate mild frosts. These can be planted into the garden several weeks before the last frost date. Consult "The Most Useful Herbs to Grow" for information on which herbs are considered hardy. Other herbs—like basil and chili peppers—are tender. These need to be hardened-off (acclimated to a new, cooler environment) in a cold frame before making the final transition from starter pot to garden soil. Inexpensive aluminum cold frames can be purchased from garden centers. These have glass lids that close over the plants at night to protect them from cold temperatures. The glass prevents frost from damaging tender plants and gradually conditions them to accept cold nights. Keep tender plants in a cold frame for 5 to 7 days.

After Care

After you prepare your soil and plant your herbs, you'll have to devise a method of controlling weeds. Though many herbs are themselves weedy-looking and are capable of competing with noxious local weeds, the garden won't look its best if you allow it to become overrun with undesirables. Some of the less aggressive annual herbs like basil, parsley, and chervil may even be suffocated by invading weeds.

The way to control weeds is to put down a 1-inch (2.5cm) layer of organic mulch, such as wood chips, cocoa bean hulls, or shredded pine bark. In addition to deterring weeds, the mulch will break down as it ages, becoming an important organic fertilizer and soil conditioner. Once mulch has broken down to the point that it is part of the soil, you will need to add another layer of mulch in order to maintain its ability to control weeds.

Another after care concern is keeping perennial herbs within their allotted spaces. In late autumn, once plants are dormant but before the ground freezes, examine perennial plants to determine whether any are growing out of bounds. If so, this is a good time to dig up overgrown clumps and divide them. Where you have some herbs of marginal hardiness (such as rosemary and lavender), pile new mulch up against the stems to protect the plants from harsh winter winds.

Wood chips make an excellent weed-suffocating mulch for herb gardens.

Watering

Most herb plants are drought-tolerant and will not need as much watering as flowers or vegetables. Some herb gardens can rely on natural rainfall to keep them healthy, but even in areas with reliable summer rainfall, there should be a water source close by for supplemental watering during dry spells. If the herb garden is small (100 square feet [9.5 sq m] or less), then it is easy to water with a common garden hose, especially one that is fitted with a watering wand, which allows you to poke the end of the hose through foliage and apply the water directly to the roots.

For a larger area, you may need to run a lawn sprinkler for several hours (like a steady rain) so that the garden gets a good soaking. It makes sense to design your herb garden so that a single oscillating sprinkler set into the middle of the garden can water the entire planting in one application without being moved around. A space 16 feet (4.8m) wide by 20 feet (6m) long can be watered efficiently by an oscillating lawn sprinkler.

A lawn sprinkler can be used to water a bed of herbs. Be careful, though—most herbs are drought-tolerant and resent over-watering.

For very large gardens, a drip irrigation system is useful, especially if your herb garden includes ornamental embellishments such as espaliered fruit trees. Avoid drip systems with nozzles and opt for those that sweat moisture along a plastic or rubber hose, since these are less prone to clogging. Usually the hose is snaked up and down rows and covered lightly with mulch, or placed beneath a layer of black plastic to protect it. One brand, Irrigro, is inexpensive enough to be used one season and discarded at the end of the season. The manufacturer also has a version that can be buried permanently. Another brand, Leaky Pipe, is made from recycled automobile tires, and can be taken up each year and stored indoors over winter to last indefinitely.

The advantage of drip systems is that an entire garden space can be watered with the turn of a faucet. Since the water is applied directly to the root zone, little is wasted from evaporation, as with overhead sprinkler systems.

Pests and Diseases

Parsley worm is actually a caterpillar. Though it is a pest on parsley, it usually does only slight damage and results in a beautiful butterfly.

You are less likely to encounter pests and diseases in herb gardens than in any other kind of garden since most herbs have developed their aromatic flavors or fragrances to repel insects or foraging animals. Indeed, many herbs—including lavender, lemongrass, lemon thyme, and wormwood—are used effectively as insect repellents,

For the healthiest garden, it is still a good policy to practice some commonsense pest and disease control. Slugs, for example, will prey on herb seedlings such as basil, and groundhogs happen to love parsley. The first line of defense is to keep your garden clean, since many insect eggs and diseases live beneath debris such as old leaves or wooden planks. Always delegate spent stems and roots of annual herbs to the compost pile, and remove old mulch from the garden at the onset of winter so slugs cannot over-winter in it. Cut the tall stems of perennial plants almost to the ground. The exceptions are semiwoody perennials like lavender, rosemary, sage, and thyme, which should be shaped, rather than heavily pruned back, to encourage a bushy habit the following season. Run a hoe between perennial plants and over fallow areas of the garden to disturb the soil and expose any dormant larvae or eggs to birds and cold. Pick up any loose boards and store them on end so that they cannot harbor pests.

Check your garden carefully in the spring; if you see the slimy silver trails of slugs, get up early in the morning and remove as many as possible with a gloved hand before they return to their hiding places. Do this several times and you will soon eliminate any slug problems.

If a groundhog or other hungry animal has a burrow nearby and is invading your garden, set a trap to capture the animal and relocate it to a forest or meadow away from busy neighborhoods. Or consider building a low fence to keep small animals out. If your problem is with deer, erect a taller fence or enclose your garden with an impenetrable hedge, such as hardy citrus.

Slugs are serious pests, and are best controlled by removal by hand or with shallow trays of slug bait, available in packages from garden centers.

Harvesting Herbs

Every herb variety has its own peak of perfection. Generally, the strongest flavors are concentrated in the youngest part of the plant. Also, the period before plants bloom, usually in late spring and early summer, is when their oils are most concentrated. For the best-tasting fresh herbs, pick them moments before you plan to use them; this is especially important for annual kinds like parsley, chervil, and basil. Many annual herbs will keep for about a day in a vase of water but their potency is diminished once they've wilted or been dried. Most perennial herbs, such as lavender, mints, and sage, react differently, and their potency is increased by drying. Pick only as much as you need, and remember that a little goes a long way.

Never denude one plant entirely. When collecting sprigs of parsley, for example, pinch a few sprigs from several different plants so that you preserve each plant's decorative qualities, and no single plant is weakened from the loss of too many leaves.

If you need to harvest a lot of different herbs at one time (as for an omelette with herbs), take a shallow basket that allows you to collect several herbs in bunches. Bring the herbs straight to the kitchen and wash them under cold running water before chopping.

Herbs that you plan to dry and store should be harvested on a dry day, since wet plants can turn moldy.

When harvesting herbs, take a few leaves from each plant so that the overall planting remains full and decorative.

Propagating Herbs

There are three ways to propagate herbs—by seeds, division, and cuttings. Annual and biennial herbs like chervil, parsley, and basil are easily propagated by seeds. Clump-forming perennial herbs like mint are most easily propagated by root division. But if the plant is bulbous, like chives, propagate it by dividing the bulblets that form around the mother bulb. Woody herbs such as lavender and scented-leaf geraniums are most successfully propagated by stem cuttings. A few herbs, like French tarragon and European hops, can be propagated by root cuttings.

Seed Starting

There are three principal seed-starting techniques for growing herbs, and the best method to use depends on the variety you are sowing. These techniques can be classified as one-step, two-step, and three-step methods.

By far the easiest is the one-step method, also known as direct seeding. This technique is best for quick-germinating annual herbs like nasturtiums, dill, and chervil.

The instructions on the seed packet will tell you whether the variety is tender or hardy and how deep to sow the seeds. Dill and chervil seedlings are hardy and can tolerate mild frosts, so seed sowing can begin several weeks before the last expected frost date in your area. Both dill and chervil will tolerate a certain amount of crowding, and are best sown thickly to form a clump. Tedious thinning to create an orderly, well-spaced row is not necessary. Cover seeds with enough soil to anchor them—usually 3 times the seed's height is adequate.

Some herbs—nasturtiums are one example—are extremely tender and should be direct-seeded only after all danger of frost is past. Consult the "The Most Useful Herbs to Grow" chapter of this book for guidance on which herbs are exceptionally tender.

When sowing directly outdoors, be sure to prepare the soil properly. Generally, herbs dislike cold or wet soil so it is best to wait until the soil surface is dry and warm. A clear plastic sheet placed over a planting bed for several days can raise the soil temperature significantly if you want to start extra early. If the soil is compacted, be sure to dig it up and break apart any thick clay clods. Rake the ground into a fine, crumbly surface by first using the tines of the rake, then by turning the rake over and using the flat metal part. Mark seed beds with labels so you will know what you sowed where.

Annual herbs like basil and most biennial herbs like parsley should be sown in spring so that you get maximum use and enjoyment from them. But hardy perennial herbs such as bee balm and chives can be sown in the summer. A summer planting allows these herbs time to form a healthy crown of leaves and a substantial root system so that they can survive winter in a dormant state.

Herb seedlings—parsley and basil are shown here beside lettuce—make strong growth in plug-type transplant pots.

The two-step method of seed starting works well with medium- and large-size seeds like basil and parsley. Since basil is sensitive to overwatering and parsley to fluctuating temperatures, start these and other temperamental plants indoors to ensure germination. Simply sow several seeds in a starter pot filled with potting soil (the first step). Then thin the resulting seedlings to the strongest one, and allow it to grow into a healthy transplant. When the seedling is 3 to 4 inches (7.5 to 10cm) high, transplant it to the garden (the second step), being careful not to disturb the roots. To avoid the mess of potting soil, you can use Jiffy-7 or Jiffy-9 peat pellets, which are made of compressed peat that expands into a pot shape when water is added. With Jiffy-7, the netting that holds the peat in place is easily torn away at transplant time to free the roots. The peat in Jiffy-9 is held together with an invisible binder, so the pot can be placed directly into the soil with no disturbance to the plant's roots.

The three-step method involves first sowing the seeds thinly into a seed tray filled with potting soil, then carefully transferring the seedlings to individual transplanting pots as soon as they are large enough to handle (usually when they are about 1 inch [2.5cm] tall). When the seedlings reach transplant size (about 4 inches [10cm] high) in their individual pots, transfer them to the garden.

With both the two-step and the three-step methods, the highest rate of germination is assured if the pots or seed trays are enclosed in a clear plastic bag to slow evaporation of moisture. Germination is also improved if the pots or seed trays are placed over a heating cable or heating mat to provide bottom heat. Most seeds germinate quickly when the soil remains at a stable 70°F (21°C) temperature.

Propagating by Division

Division is the easiest way to propagate most perennial herbs, including those that produce bulbs, such as chives and saffron. Most perennial herbs produce vigorous root systems that can be dug up and divided after they have established a healthy clump (usually in the second or third season). After digging up the root system, it is best to use a strong jet of water from a hose to wash away the soil, and then use a trowel to pry apart the roots. Most root masses will come apart easily once the soil is washed away, with a healthy crown of stems or leaves on top of each division. Root masses with many different-size roots may be more

These divisions of orris root are ready to be replanted in the garden. Plants are easily divided once the roots have been washed of excess soil.

difficult to divide and you may have to use a sharp knife. You'll then end up with a mixture of large and small divisions. The large divisions can be planted directly into the garden where you want

Divisions of lemongrass (center) can be transplanted to make new plants. The cut sections (bottom) are excellent brewed as an herbal tea.

the plants to mature. The smaller divisions can be potted-up and held in a cold frame to increase in size, or delegated to a special nursery bed to size-up.

With bulbous plants, division is even easier. All you need to do after digging up the clump is to wash away the soil; the bulblets will almost fall away from the parent bulb by themselves. Again, you will be able to separate the bulblets into small and large sizes. The large bulbs will be able to fend for themselves in the garden, while the smaller bulbs are better transferred to individual pots or a nursery bed to increase in size before they are planted in the garden.

Propagating by Cuttings

There are several types of cuttings that can be taken from plants, including stem cuttings, root cuttings, and leaf cuttings. The methods most often used to propagate herbs are stem cuttings and root cuttings.

Two herbs that are easy to propagate from stem cuttings are lavender and scented-leaf geraniums. Simply select a healthy plant and cut a 5- or 6-inch (13 or 15cm) section from any healthy stem or branch. Cut on a slant just below a leaf node, preferably using a branch tip. If there are any flowers or seed pods on the cutting, remove them. Then strip away half the leaves from the bottom section of the cutting and dip the cut end into a rooting hormone.

When taking stem cuttings, you simply strip the leaves from the bottom portion of the stem, dip the cut stem into rooting hormone, and stick it into potting soil.

Rooted cuttings of lavender are ready for transplanting to the garden after danger of frost has passed.

Rooting hormones are usually sold in a powder form (which looks like flour) at garden centers. Tap out a little of the rooting hormone into a saucer and use that to dip into, rather than dipping the stem directly into the container. This keeps the hormone in the container clean for subsequent applications.

Next, stick the cut end of the treated cuttings into a seed tray filled with moist potting soil. Arrange the cuttings in straight rows spaced at least 3 inches (7.5cm) apart, or cluster them around the edges of a clay pot. Wrap the entire seed tray or pot in a clear plastic wrap, creating a dome over the cuttings, and place it in a warm, brightly lit place. The plastic helps to reduce evaporation.

It's possible to take root cuttings from herbs with aggressive, stoloniferous root systems such as mints and horseradish. Simply dig up a root ball, wash away the excess soil with water, and cut sections of root with a node, or growing point. The root cuttings should be about 2 inches (5cm) long. Simply place the root onto a peat-based potting soil and cover it lightly, with the node pointing up. Within several weeks the root section will produce new feeder roots underneath the node, while the node itself will elongate into a green growing shoot.

Most cuttings will begin to sprout new roots in 2 to 3 weeks. In any case, remove the plastic cover and examine the cuttings at 2-week intervals. When roots have developed and are at least 1 inch (2.5cm) long, the cuttings can be transferred to small individual pots to size-up (such as 3-inch [7.5cm] plastic or peat pots). When roots poke through the drainage hole in the pots (or penetrate the walls of the peat pots) the cuttings can be safely transplanted to the garden. If there is still chance of frost outside, harden-off the transplants first by placing them in a cold frame.

Herb Garden
Themes
and Designs

Opposite: A vintage cart full of potted herbs makes a charming display.

Designing with herbs is not nearly as easy as planning a flower garden. Though many herbs (like lavender and bee balm) have extremely beautiful flowers, making it possible to imitate a mixed perennial border with them, others have small or inconspicuous flowers. In growing these herbs we must compensate for the lack of color with a strong, imaginative design that emphasizes other qualities such as plant habit (the low carpeting effect of thyme or the tall, elegant branching of dill) and leaf shape, color, and texture.

The first consideration is whether to choose a formal or an informal design. Generally, a pleasing formal layout is easier to achieve with herbs, because the geometry of a formal layout can compensate for lack of color.

For a formal look, consider a knot garden, a parterre, a quadrant design, or a cartwheel design, with the lines of the planting area outlined by trimmed hedges of boxwood, germander, sage, or lavender cotton. The herbs within the sharply defined beds can be planted in blocks and spaced in a diamond pattern to keep the design clean and crisp.

Vining Plants

There are not many vining herbs that are useful for home gardeners, but there are several hardy annual and perennial plants that are not out of place in most herb gardens because they have edible parts. Perhaps the most useful is the European hop vine, which produces lime green, papery fruits and ivy-shaped leaves. The fruit are used to introduce a characteristic bitter flavor to beer; they are also beautiful in herbal wreaths and dried arrangements. Hops are best grown from cuttings using part of their vigorous underground root system.

Other vining plants to consider are annual climbing nasturtiums (see page 98); the purple-podded hyacinth bean; scarlet runner beans, which have beautiful red flower clusters followed by long, flat edible beans; and any fragrant old climbing rose such as 'Zephirine Drouhin' (shown here).

Mixing Herbs with Flowers

You don't need to create a special herb garden to grow a wide assortment of herbs. Many herbs can be placed among annuals and perennials in flower beds and borders. Some hardy varieties include anise hyssop, bee balm, chives, lavender, and parsley. You can also add tender herbs to your flower beds by growing them in pots that can be moved indoors for the winter. Just sink the pots into the soil after the last frost, and these herbs will blend successfully with the ornamental aspects of your garden. Some particularly beautiful herbs to grow in a flower bed include: lemongrass (its 3-foot [90cm], arching, grassy leaf blades create a fountain-like effect, shining yellow when backlit by the sun); cinnamon basil (its dark purple stems, lustrous dark green leaves, and light purple flower spikes are outstanding among flowering plants); and scented-leaf geraniums (which not only possess unusual leaf shapes and textures, but also interesting flowers among some varieties).

If you prefer an informal look, consider planting your herbs like a small meadow. You can still plan a simple layout of paths leading through the planting, but instead of defined blocks of herbs, create a tapestry of foliage effects in a mix of shapes and heights. Additional interest can be introduced with rocky outcrops, an old farm implement like a hand plow, or a rustic split-rail fence among the herbs.

Beds and Borders

Many herbs not only possess culinary value, but are also decorative and useful as flowering plants for landscaping in a bed or border. A particularly good bed shape to use is the kidney form, which can be surrounded by lawn or flagstone. For the best effect, arrange plants in tiers—tall plants in the middle, intermediate-height plants next, and low-spreading plants as an edging.

Borders are usually butted against a structure, such as a wall, fence, or hedge, so it is better to place tall plants at the back, intermediate-height plants in the middle, and low plants at the front. Stepping stones can be used in both beds and borders to make it easier to harvest the herbs.

Some particularly good flowering plants to use in beds and borders are anise hyssop, bee balm, catmint, chamomile, chives, dill, garlic chives, lavender, marigolds, nasturtiums, and thyme. It is not necessary to use the same number of plants for each herb you wish to plant. Indeed, you'll get a much more beautiful effect if certain flowering herbs are allowed to dominate. For instance, you might use a mass of dill as a tall background plant, clumps of lavender or chives as an intermediate-height plant, and swathes of thyme as an edging.

In beds and borders, herbs with colorful foliage can be very effective, since from a distance these brilliant leaves are highly ornamental. Some examples of herbs with decorative foliage are golden oregano, tricolor sage, purple basil, silver lavender cotton, and blue-foliaged rue.

Because nearly all herbs thrive in soil with excellent drainage, herb beds and borders benefit from raising the soil level as much as possible. Using boulders or thick tree limbs as an edging for your bed or border will give you a pleasing, natural look that also promotes improved drainage.

A decorative mulch for weed control is advisable. My personal favorite is shredded pine bark because it is so attractive and does not deteriorate as quickly as other organic matter like grass clippings and pine needles.

Beehive Garden

Beehives are not only useful for housing the bees that help to pollinate plants and manufacture honey, they can also serve as a decorative accent in herb gardens where a focal point is needed. There are many styles of beehive, some of which contribute a quaint air to the garden, such as old-fashioned bee skeps, which are wicker, cone-shaped beehives. Avoid the beehives constructed of grass or thatching, as they can fall apart after just one season. Bee skeps are at their best shellacked to resist rotting and placed on a low pedestal. Usually, paths radiate from the beehive, forming

In this lush, somewhat chaotic planting, an old-fashioned beehive adds a whimsical touch. A small-space medieval-style herb garden can be made to look authentic with the simple addition of a beehive. In a formal garden the hive makes an admirable central accent.

pie-shaped beds that can be filled with herbs. These beds can be planted in an orderly fashion and outlined with low braided wicker fences to create a formal, medieval appearance, or the herbs can be encouraged to knit into each other and spill into the pathways for a more informal look.

Butterfly and Hummingbird Garden

A modern alternative to the beehive garden is a garden that uses mostly flowering herbs to attract butterflies and hummingbirds. Butterflies are highly attracted to the flowers of basil, oregano, and mint; tubular red flowers such as those of pineapple sage, bee balm, and nasturtiums are a magnet for hummingbirds. As an additional attraction to hummingbirds, be sure to include in your garden a variety of trumpet creeper (also known as hummingbird vine). Try either the common *Campsis radicans* or the hybrid variety 'Madam Galen', which has larger flowers and stays in bloom longer. Though lacking herbal qualities, this vine makes a lovely complement to an herb garden, and there is nothing in all the floral kingdom more certain to attract hummingbirds.

Quadrant Garden

This herb garden executed in a quadrant design features plantings outlined in lavender cotton. Even very small spaces can be effectively planted using a quadrant plan.

The quadrant design is the oldest and most popular way to display herbs. It is simply a rectangular or square space with a path cutting the area into four equal, or nearly equal, parts. The quadrant is usually outlined by a fence, with a perimeter border inside the fence planted with perennial herbs—such as horseradish, mints, chives, rhubarb, and lemon balm. The inner squares are mainly

This traditional herb design, popular in Colonial gardens, features a rectangle of different-colored thymes planted as a "quilt." Brick paths surround this central bed, as well as four additional planting spaces outlined by parterres of silvery lavender cotton. The entire garden is defined by a boxwood hedge.

A   Varieties of thyme: pink, white, red, purple-flowered

B   English lavender

C   Bee balm

D   Chives

E   Spearmint

F   Cinnamon basil

G   Fennel

H   Lemongrass

I   Rue

J   Dill

K   Tarragon

L   Rosemary

M   Chamomile

N   Orris

O   Lovage

P   Marjoram

Q   Lemon balm

R   Parsley

S   Horehound

T   Sage

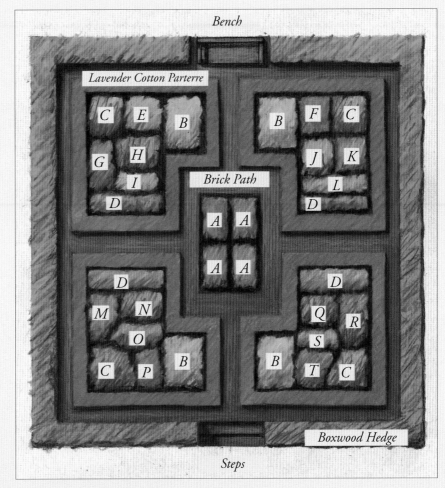

used to grow annual herbs and vegetables—parsley, basil, dill, beans, tomatoes, and peppers, for example. The quadrants are useful for crop rotation of annual plants that are especially prone to diseases. Growing families of plants in a different bed each year reduces the risk of disease and ensures maximum vigor.

Though quadrants can be rather plain in design, embellishment can be provided by edging each quadrant with a low hedge of chives and thyme, using a decorative paving for the paths (amber-colored pea gravel is especially attractive), and by choosing an ornament, such as a dovecote, for the center of the quadrant.

Cartwheel Garden

This classic herb garden design dates back at least to the Elizabethan period. It is similar to the quadrant design, except the perimeter is circular and the beds are pie-shaped, defined by paths or hedge dividers that radiate like the spokes of a wheel from a central point. Often, the center of the design features an ornamental element, such as a birdbath or a sundial, at the center of the garden. The paths are usually gravel—to create an authentic Elizabethan look—or brick or flagstone for a Colonial-style garden.

Upended bricks define the pie-shaped beds, while flat bricks create the paths in this formal herb garden. A low hedge of dwarf boxwood borders the entire space, which, despite its circular elements, is laid out on a square. You can easily dispense with the outer portion of the design if a circular planting better suits your garden space. A garden of this type is made complete with a central accent—a statue, birdbath, or small pool is an ideal focal point for the center bed.

A	**English lavender**
B	**Parsley**
C	**Horehound**
D	**Burnet**
E	**Chives**
F	**Spearmint**
G	**Tarragon**
H	**Bee balm**
I	**Angelica**
J	**Rosemary**
K	**Sage**
L	**Rue**
M	**Cinnamon basil**
N	**Lemon basil**
O	**Green curled basil**
P	**Purple curled basil**
Q	**English thyme**
R	**Chamomile**
S	**Orris**
T	**Lovage**
U	**Marjoram**
V	**Fennel**
W	**Lemongrass**
X	**Dill**
Y	**Marigold 'Gem'**

Above: Cartwheel designs feature paths radiating out from a hub, creating a pie-shaped arrangement of beds. While this cartwheel is rather elaborate, you can simplify the design to fit your space. Below: White flowers echo the paintwork on a dovecote and gazebo. Garden features painted white will accentuate the glowing quality of white flowers.

Small and creative cartwheel designs can be made using a rusty old iron tractor wheel laid on its side. Large cartwheel designs are often quite elaborate, using wheels within wheels.

Color Theme Garden

Many herbs have conspicuous flowers, and, interestingly, the predominant bloom colors of herbs are pink and white. This is so overwhelmingly true that it is possible to plant a color theme garden of entirely pink flowers, or to design an all-white herb garden. You could also combine the pink and white types, since these two colors go very well together.

To help establish the color theme, it is usually desirable to have some decorative structures in the garden, such as a

Silver in the Herb Garden

Since many herbs have silvery leaves—artemisia, lavender, sage, and santolina for example—it's fairly easy to create a romantic silver garden. The glittering effect of these herbs is enhanced when they are planted with white-flowering herbs like white valerian, white bee balm, white varieties of thyme, white garlic chives, white lavender, and white yarrow. Silver and white gardens are especially beautiful in the moonlight, when the plants reflect the moon's glow.

gazebo or birdhouses, painted in the theme colors. To carry color above the height of most culinary herbs, plant fragrant white or pink wisteria or climbing roses in the same blush colors. These plants are perfectly at home in the herb garden, since the blossoms of both are used in making perfumes and potpourris.

Dyer's woodruff (*Asperula tinctoria*) grows in profusion on this Pennsylvania farm. Relatively large plots are necessary to produce the volume of plant material required for a usable amount of dye.

Dyer's Garden

Dyer's gardens are intended for growing the herbs traditionally used to color textiles. The main problem in growing this type of garden is that you generally need a lot of a particular dye plant to make even a little dye. Therefore, most dye gardens resemble cut-flower gardens, with specific dye plants placed in wide straight rows and a walkway running between each row for easy access. Rather than planting large dye gardens of their own, many dyers concentrate on just a few dye plants and look to wayside plants as a source of material. Such common weeds as Queen Anne's lace (a source of green dye) and goldenrod (a source of yellow dye) are easily gathered from sunny wildflower meadows.

Materials for dyeing, in addition to the dye plant, include wool, water, and a mordant (a metallic salt, like chrome, copper, or alum, used to fix the color). The ingredients are all combined in a pot to simmer—a simple enough procedure. The tricky part is knowing the right formula for each batch of wool, since the amount of wool, dye plant, and mordant will differ according to the type of dye plants available and the type of mordant used. For more information on dyeing, refer to the reading list at the end of this book (page 118).

Fragrance Garden

Since almost all herbs are fragrant to some degree, it may seem redundant to separate them for fragrance. But the fact is that some herbs are more pleasantly fragrant than others. By choosing the right kinds of herbs, a fragrant herb garden can be made using only a few plants. Indeed, I have often seen a corner of a garden planted with just two plant families— lavender and scented-leaf geraniums. In my own garden the stems and leaves from

Lavender Lore

There is much confusion in lavender nomenclature. English lavender is *Lavandula angustifolia*, sometimes called *L. vera* or *L. officinalis*. The two most popular varieties of lavender are 'Munstead' (a mid-blue) and 'Hidcote' (a violet-blue). The lavender of Provence is *L. × intermedia* 'Grosso', a hybrid of English lavender. All of these varieties are relatively hardy.

Then there is a wide range of fairly similar tender lavenders, collectively known as Mediterranean lavenders, which includes *L. stoechas* (Italian lavender), *L. dentata* (French lavender), and *L. pedunculata* (Spanish lavender). Most of these plants have a purple or pink coloration

and tufts of wavy petals that are especially beautiful when backlit. There is also a lovely green-flowering lavender, *L. viridis*, with a scent reminiscent of pine and lavender. Except in areas with fairly mild winters, these Mediterranean lavenders are best grown in containers and moved indoors during winter.

these two plants grow through a wrought-iron bench so that the aromas of lavender, plus coconut, lemon, and rose from the geraniums, pervade the atmosphere every time I sit down.

In addition to scenting the garden, fragrant herbs are useful in potpourri (see pages 61-62 for more information on potpourri), scented sachets, and scented pillows. How

Chocolate Mint

In almost all herb families there are special varieties worth cultivating above all others. Among mints, 'Chocolate Mint' is a case in point. Discovered many years ago in Mitcham, England, 'Chocolate Mint' smells like chocolate, and when dried even tastes like chocolate. It is easy to grow—even on windowsills—and it is extremely hardy.

'Chocolate Mint' resembles spearmint, but it is more compact and the stems have a chocolate brown coloration. The glossy leaves are spear-shaped, with a bronze sheen. The flowers, which open in the summer, are dainty and are held above the foliage on purple spikes. The leaves have a distinct 'chocolate mint' aroma.

The 'Chocolate Mint' plant is hardy and will grow anywhere in North America from Canada to Florida, coast to coast. It tolerates heat, poor soil, and even crowded conditions, making it useful as a decorative groundcover. Unlike spearmint or peppermint, it is not a rampant grower and can easily be controlled by simply trimming the edges. Brushing against the leaves or bruising them releases the fragrance. One of my favorite places to grow 'Chocolate Mint' is close to a lawn where the mower blades can cut into the leaves to fill the garden with fragrance.

Place 'Chocolate Mint' in full sun or light shade. A good way to grow it is in a pot in a sunny window, where it is easy to pick a leaf and enjoy its pleasant aroma. Chop a leaf up and add it to cakes, cookies, desserts, and drinks for a minty flavor. Chop it fine and use it for a flavoring over ice cream, over a mixed fruit salad, and in a cup of hot chocolate. Drying 'Chocolate Mint' intensifies the chocolate aroma, making it a good choice for potpourri.

Lawns of Chamomile and Thyme

There is a species of chamomile known botanically by two names: *Chamaemelum nobile*, and *Anthemis nobilis*. A common name for this plant is Roman chamomile (as opposed to German chamomile). Though Roman chamomile appears similar to German chamomile, with small, white, daisylike flowers and yellow button centers, it does not grow

as tall, and usually stays under 6 inches (15cm) in height, making it an ideal groundcovering.

A special form of Roman chamomile, called 'Treneague', produces a low, dense weave of fernlike leaves suitable for growing as a lawn. This variety usually does not flower—especially if it is mowed—and if it does bloom, the flowers are incomplete, composed only of button centers without white petals. 'Treneague' is a tender perennial that prefers mild winters. Where it can survive the winter, it makes an unusual fragrant lawn that can take a lot of wear and tear.

There are many varieties of low, spreading thyme. These differ in the color of their flowers (which bloom in colors from white and pale pink to deep pink, red, and purple) and their foliage (which ranges from various shades of green to silver and gold). You can use one color alone to create a low groundcover effect, or mix the varieties so that they form a patchwork of different colors. Both the low creeping forms of chamomile and thyme are excellent for sunny, dry slopes, where it is difficult to use a lawn mower.

delightful it is to pick a simple sprig of lavender from the garden and place it beside a pillow to produce the sensation of waking up in a wildflower meadow! Rose petals, too, have the power to fill a room with fragrance. A combination of roses and lavender is often the basis of the most popular potpourri. But be aware that many modern roses lack fragrance. In the quest to breed for size and special colors, fragrance is often the first quality to be sacrificed. It is, therefore, essential to know precisely which roses produce

Planted Walls and Paving

There are many kinds of herbs that thrive in dry walls and between cracks in paving. It is possible to have a paved area entirely filled with herbal plants. As the paving is walked over, the aromatic leaves become bruised and the volatile oils are released to fill the air with a spicy fragrance. One of the best herbs to plant in between paving stones is creeping thyme. But be sure to choose varieties that have fragrance, since some creeping thymes are not aromatic. The most fragrant thymes include English thyme (*Thymus vulgaris*) and its many cultivars, as well as lemon thyme (*T.* x *citriodorus*). Here are some other good contenders:

• Chamomile • Cheddar pinks • Chives • Curry plant • Signet marigolds • Lamb's ears •

• Dwarf nasturtiums • Creeping forms of oregano, such as 'Aurea'

• Green and silver santolina • Violas

Most of these will even grow out of cracks in vertical walls, if the wall has ample pockets to hold soil and plants.

worthwhile scents. 'La Reine Victoria' and 'Apothecary's Rose' are two beautifully scented possibilities.

It's important to devise ways for the plants to release their fragrances, since many will do so only by being crushed or bruised. Besides allowing herbs to grow through a bench, as described earlier, consider placing low-growing, fragrant herbs where they will be walked on; each footstep will bruise the leaves and release their oils. Creeping varieties of thyme and chamomile are excellent for this technique, since these low-spreading, aromatic plants can be planted between cracks in paving and flagstone. Indeed, it is said that the more they are trod upon the stronger they grow!

Thyme is such a durable, drought-resistant, ground-hugging plant that it can be used for a special lawn effect, with different colors laid out like a quilt design. Many gardens cry out for a comfortable section of slope on which you can stretch out and admire a view. Grass is attractive, but rather mundane, while thyme has the advantage of providing both a cushion-soft texture and a wonderful aroma.

Knot Garden

These two knot gardens, one in the shape of a star, are connected by a lavender-edged path. A fence full of climbing roses separates the garden spaces.

Among all the garden designs used to display herbs, the knot garden is unique, and it is the most readily recognizable form of herb garden. Knot gardens are usually composed of low hedges of perennial herbs with contrasting leaf colors—like glossy green germander, bronze-leaf barberry, or silvery lavender cotton—laid out in a pattern. The spaces between the hedges contain either a mass planting of a particular herb or a collection of herbs, although sometimes the planting beds are alternated with a colored gravel to enhance the decorative effect of the design.

Knot gardens are best located in a sunken area, where the beauty of the design can be fully appreciated, or placed below an elevated observation place, such as a terrace, balcony, or small hill.

Parterre

The word *parterre* is French for "on the ground," and parterres are similar to knot gardens. The knot garden, however, is usually more elaborate, with the hedges of different varieties crisscrossing to appear as though they are knotted. Parterres can be much simpler in design, and are often planted with a single hedge material in a pattern; the spaces in between are then planted with herbs of different colors. As with knot gardens, parterres are best located in areas where they can be viewed from above.

This beautiful French parterre garden recalls the contemplative quality of gardens at medieval monasteries. Vine-covered walls ensure privacy and enhance the feeling of quiet serenity.

Single-Plant Theme Garden

A mint garden is divided and contained by the use of landscape ties—each compartment features a different variety. Because mint tends to run rampant, this is an excellent way to keep it from overreaching its bounds. The old-fashioned water pump makes a charming and useful accent for an herb planting.

Certain classes of herbs have a large number of varieties, especially basil, lavender, mint, and scented-leaf geraniums. These plant theme gardens need not be large to be appealing. Basil, for example, has a cushion-shaped cultivar called 'Green Mound' that resembles dwarf boxwood and can be used as a low edging. Two tall, ruffle-leafed basils, 'Green Ruffles' and 'Purple Ruffles', add strong decorative accents. There are also several free-flowering basil cultivars, among them 'Cinnamon', which has dark stems, attractive shiny bronze leaves, and pink flowers.

Hardy English lavender varieties and cultivars include a white-flowered type, along with several shades of blue, while the more tender French and Spanish types also come in various shades of pink.

Mints are a particularly good plant group to work with because they are so useful. Not only are there different green leaf forms of peppermint and spearmint, but also attractive color variations among the perfumed mints, such as apple mint, orange mint, and 'Eau de Cologne' mint—all of which are suitable for making refreshing teas. The design for an all-mint garden should, however, take into consideration that they can spread aggressively, blurring the boundaries between your different types of mint and overtaking the rest of the garden as well. Define your mint beds to prevent this rampant grower from spreading too far—boards sunk 1 foot (30cm) or so below ground level work well.

Physic Garden

The Physick Garden at the University of British Columbia in Canada features herbs that have medicinal value. Today, medical researchers are taking a new look at traditional healing herbs and evaluating them for contemporary use.

Also called a physick garden, a physic garden is a place where medicinal plants are grown. Before the manufacture of modern drugs and medicines, herbs were used for the relief of many ailments. Monasteries usually had a special area for the growing of medicinal herbs. Indeed, 25 percent of prescription pharmaceuticals are still derived from plants, and even today there are many parts of the world (particularly China) where herbs are considered the best form of healing. There are hospitals and historic institutions today that maintain elaborate physic gardens, either for continued research into healing through herbs, or for ornamental value and links to the past.

Apart from the inclusion of herbs, shrubs, and trees used in healing, the other common element of physic gardens is a formal design. Outlined with cobblestone, gravel, or brick paths, the design usually features a statue of a famous scientist or physician as a focal point.

Physic gardens are invariably enclosed by a high wall or impenetrable hedge, because many of the plants used in medicine are poisonous when not used appropriately. These include foxgloves (which can be used to control the heartbeat) and monkshood (used in the relief of toothache).

Container Garden

Herbs are particularly well suited for growing in containers because one plant of any herb is usually sufficient for flavoring meals. A convenient place to grow a few potted herbs is a sunny kitchen windowsill, where the plants are handy for the picking of a few sprigs of this or that. Container gardening with herbs is a good way to pack a lot of plants into a small space, especially if you have no soil—all you need is a sunny spot: a wooden deck or a brick patio is perfect. Even ungainly or tall herbs like dill will generally grow shorter when confined to a pot. And, since many herbs are drought-tolerant, they will thrive with less watering than most ornamental annuals and perennials.

Some good containers for growing herbs are clay pots, urns, windowsill planters, and strawberry planters, which are urn-shaped vessels with planting pockets all over the surface of the pot. Some herbs, such as vining nasturtiums and bushy parsley, are even suitable for growing in hanging baskets. Wire baskets lined with moist sphagnum moss over solid plastic dry out less quickly than other baskets, and the herbs can be poked through the sides to completely cover the container.

A rule of thumb: the bigger the pot, the better it is for growing herbs. Most herbs have vigorous root systems that benefit from a roomy container, which encourages them to produce a bushy plant, while small containers (less than 1-gallon [3.7L] capacity) tend to dry out too quickly. Avoid containers with poor insulation, like those made of plastic or metal. These can overheat quickly and burn tender feeder roots. Far better are ceramic or wooden containers (especially wooden whiskey half-barrels) since these keep roots cool.

In larger pots, try planting herbs in a variety of heights, so that a tall herb like lemongrass gives the arrangement stature, while spreading herbs like oregano and thyme can cascade over the lip of the container.

Lemongrass contributes a lovely fountain effect to this potted garden. Many herbs will grow quite satisfactorily in containers placed in a sunny corner of a deck, patio, or courtyard.

Some herbs, like rosemary and bay, can be trained into tree forms and grown as topiary—a wooden Versailles planter or an ornate clay pot enhances the display. Although these tree-form herbs may be too tender for northern gardens, they can be moved inside to survive the winter.

Fragrant herbs make an excellent choice for a potted dooryard garden. Here, sorrel and scented-leaf geraniums, among other plants, grace an entryway at historic Conestoga House in Pennsylvania.

To provide good anchorage for vigorous herbs like lavender and rosemary, I always use a premixed potting soil with some garden topsoil or loam soil added. Although there are premixed potting soils specifically made for filling containers, these tend to be peat-based and lightweight. A good homemade, general-purpose potting mix should

consist of equal parts of garden topsoil, construction sand (not beach sand), and peat. Also add a general-purpose granular fertilizer to provide extra nutrients and some perlite, which aids in retaining moisture.

Water the container whenever the soil surface feels dry, and choose a sunny location for your pot. Herbs are not greedy feeders and a weak foliar feeding (via a liquid fertilizer spray applied to the leaves) once a month is generally sufficient to keep them healthy. Most important is good drainage. If the container has a drainage hole, be sure to place some wire, stones, or pieces of broken crockery over the hole to prevent its becoming clogged or compacted with soil.

Mulch the soil surface of containers with a decorative organic material such as bark chips, cocoa bean hulls, or landscape chips to prevent rapid moisture evaporation. This is especially important in hanging baskets, which tend to dry out more quickly than any other type of container. If there is no drainage hole and it's not possible to drill one (as with a stone trough), then create a drainage field of crushed stones at the base of the container before adding the potting soil. If excessive watering or rain waterlogs the container, tilt it so the excess water pours out.

Here is a list of herbs that are especially good for growing in containers:
Bay laurel (*Laurus nobilis*)
'Blue Mound' rue (*Ruta graveolens* 'Blue Mound')
'Chocolate Mint' (*Mentha* × *piperita* 'Chocolate Mint')
Common chives (*Allium schoenoprasum*)
English lavender (*Lavandula angustifolia*)
'Extra Curly Dwarf' parsley (*Petroselium crispum* 'Extra Dwarf Curly')
Garlic chives (*Allium tuberosum*)
'Golden' oregano (*Origanum vulgare* 'Golden')
'Green Globe' basil (*Ocimum basilicum* 'Green Globe')
'Hidcote' lavender (*Lavandula angustifolia* 'Hidcote')
Lemongrass (*Cymbopogon citratum*)
Lemon thyme (*Thymus* × *citriodorus*)
Nasturtiums (*Tropoealum majus*)
Prostrate rosemary (*Rosmarinus officinalis* 'Prostrata')
'Rose-Scented' geranium (*Pelargonium* 'Rose-Scented')
'Tricolor' sage (*Salvia officinalis* 'Tricolor')

Using
Herbs

Opposite: An herbal wreath decorates the door of a cottage at Cedaridge Farm. In this cottage is the room we use for drying herbs—the wreath serves as a pretty signpost!

Many herbs are used fresh from the garden, either as a garnish (like parsley and chives) or as an infusion to make refreshing tea (like lavender and mints). However, many more herbs (including those we use fresh) can be easily preserved by drying or freezing, and the flavor of some herbs is actually intensified by drying.

Herbs are among the most gratifying plants to grow because they often have multiple purposes—flavoring food, scenting the air, and pleasing the eye.

Store dried leaves and petals for potpourris in airtight, screw-top jars to preserve their aromas. Do be sure that the petals are thoroughly dried before putting them in jars, though; if there is any moisture left they will begin to mold.

Fresh Herbs

Herbs are used so often in the kitchen that it pays to consider ways of having them available fresh all the time. Some obvious places to grow culinary herbs include a raised bed beside the kitchen door or in a collection of pots on a deck or patio.

Indoors, space can sometimes be found on sunny windowsills. If you don't get enough hours of sunlight in any of your windows, try growing some treasured herbs under grow lights.

Certain herbs are almost synonymous with particular foods: chopped mint for perking up fruit salad or iced tea and in mint sauce over lamb; horseradish for spicing up beef; rosemary to enhance the flavor of chicken; sage for turkey stuffing; and basil to add a desirable piquancy to tomato sauce. In the culinary arts, matching the right herb or combination of herbs to the right meal is the essence of fine dining, whether the course being prepared is a salad, soup, entree, or dessert. Some of the best herb partnerships are: parsley and chives in an omelette; basil and chili peppers in a pesto sauce; dill and tarragon with fish or chicken; and rosemary and thyme in a meat sauce. For a sensational flavor enhancer on fruit salad try finely chopped mint and a dash of cinnamon.

Edible Flowers

Many of the common herbs featured in this book have edible flowers, including borage, chives, marigolds, and nasturtiums. However, there are many other plants not normally considered herbs that also have delicious flowers. Since these edible flowers can be used for decoration or to brighten up salads, it makes sense to include them in legitimate herb gardens. My personal favorites include:

• Calendulas • Carnations

• Chrysanthemums • Hibiscus

• Hollyhocks • Malvas

• Violets • Yucca

When using flowers as an edible garnish, be sure to wash them first, as you would any salad ingredient.

This "thyme clock" is planted with different varieties of thyme, which can be easily harvested for culinary use. The visual pun adds an enchanting aspect to the herb garden.

The best restaurants all have herb gardens on the premises or they have arranged for fresh herbs to be delivered daily from a local herb garden. It is simply not possible to prepare true gourmet meals without the enhancement of fresh herbs. Herbs add zest, scent, and beauty to otherwise ordinary dishes. Simple salads, for example, acquire amazing flavors when a few fresh herbs are tossed in. Some invaluable fresh garnishes for salads include parsley, chives, basil, thyme, tarragon, and dill, either chopped fine, mixed as an herbal vinegar, or prepared as an herbal dressing.

When flavoring soups, it's best to match the herb to the base of the stock. Parsley and dill are especially good for adding to seafood bisques and chowders. Chives, basil, and oregano work wonders for vegetable soups, while rocket, watercress, and sorrel add both an appealing green color and a bittersweet flavor to mild soups like potato, onion, and navy bean.

Drying Herbs

Drying herbs in the sun bleaches out more of the leaves' color than drying them in the dark, and at the same time weakens any aromatic properties. A dark attic or barn is an excellent place to dry herbs, as is a warm, dry, dark utility closet, or any other dry dark space.

Good ventilation is vital; otherwise the herbs are likely to rot. A small fan can be used to improve the air circulation.

The easiest way to dry herbs with aromatic stems or leaves is to simply gather the stems together at the base, hold them in place with a rubber band or twist-tie, and hang them from a rafter. This is especially good for herbs that you plan to use in potpourri, such as sweet Annie and scented-leaf geraniums. If you don't have rafters, hang the herbs from a clothes rack or on a line strung between walls. It's also easy to dry herbs by clumping them upright in manila envelopes attached to a wall or laid flat on newspapers in the back of a station wagon, where the sun can shine through the window and dry them as if they were in a greenhouse.

Some herbs (like anise and dill) have aromatic seeds that need to be shucked from their seed capsules when dry. The easiest way to do this is to tie a paper bag over the upturned seed head so the seeds are collected in the bag. Once dried, herbs can be stored indefinitely in airtight, screw-top glass jars.

Once herbs have been dried, their leaves, stems, and petals may be crushed very fine with a mortar and pestle and stored in airtight jars.

Freezing Herbs

Herbs that have been frozen retain an amazing amount of their fresh flavor. Usually, they need to be chopped and stored in plastic freezer bags. An advantage of freezing herbs over drying is that frozen herbs generally retain their color (though they will lose their shape and texture) and look much fresher than the dried product. Also, many culinary herbs—such as parsley, basil, and dill—simply don't store well when dried. To freeze these herbs, spread the leaves onto a cookie sheet and place the sheet in the freezer. After freezing, remove them, crumble them with your fingers, and store them in the freezer in a freezer bag.

Another method is to chop the herbs and place them into freezer bags and freeze them in the bags. Be aware that freezing basil turns it an unappealing black color, but it does not harm the flavor. Another great way to freeze herbs is to chop them up, place them in an ice cube tray, fill the tray with water, then freeze. When the cubes are frozen put them in a freezer bag. The chopped herbs are suspended in the ice, and are protected from being crushed in the freezer. For soups and sauces that won't be affected by the water, I just throw the cubes in; for other dishes I run the cubes under cool water until the ice melts.

Basil Pesto

Here's my favorite pesto recipe:

Ingredients

   1½ cups of fresh basil leaves, washed and dried

   2 tablespoons of virgin olive oil

   3 tablespoons of garlic or basil herb vinegar

   3 tablespoons of pine nuts

   2 cloves of chopped garlic

   ½ teaspoon of salt

   ¼ teaspoon ground pepper

   ½ cup of chopped parsley

   ¼ cup of chopped chives or garlic chives

   1 cup of parmesan cheese

Place the oil, vinegar, pine nuts, garlic, salt, and pepper into a food processor or a blender. Add the basil leaves, parsley, and chives and blend until creamy. Pour the mixture into a bowl and stir in the parmesan. Stir the pesto into freshly cooked, drained pasta, adding melted butter if desired.

Herbal Butters and Pestos

Herbal butters are an excellent way to flavor your foods with herbs. Simply chop some culinary herbs like garlic chives and parsley into a pat of melted butter and freeze it until you want to use the herbal butter as a toast spread, for basting, or in a sauce. Usually, butter to be used on toast requires less of the herb than if the butter is to be used for basting, since a little of an herb can go a long way.

Pestos are made from pureed basil and a combination of other ingredients such as garlic, virgin olive oil, and salt. However, it's worth experimenting with rosemary, sage, and parsley as the main ingredient.

Herbal Teas

The flavor of some herbs is best released in liquids. For example, Earl Grey tea is made from the leaves of bee balm, also called bergamot. Stimulating hot drinks are also made from ginseng root, lavender leaves, mint, chamomile, lemongrass, and rose-scented geraniums. For a particularly refreshing summer drink, fill a small muslin bag with mint leaves and let it steep in lemon-flavored iced tea.

The aromatic dried leaves of mint make a refreshing, caffeine-free tea.

Herbal vinegars in glass bottles make a beguiling display in the window of a shop.

Vinegars

Herbal vinegars are not only excellent flavor enhancers for salads, they can also be highly decorative embellishments to a kitchen when stored in fancy glass bottles. It is easy to make herbal vinegar: thoroughly wash and dry the herbs and put them into a glass jar with a tight-fitting lid; pour vinegar (make sure it has 5 percent acidity) over the herbs, seal the jar tightly, and set it in a cool, dark place. Shake the jar up every few days. After 2 or 3 weeks, strain the vinegar into a stainless steel pan and bring it to a boil. Put a sprig or two of the chosen herb into a sterilized bottle or jar and pour the hot vinegar into the bottle, leaving ½ inch (1.5cm) of room at the top. Seal, cool, and store in a cool, dark place. Vinegars prepared this way will keep for up to 3 months. For a decorative touch, label the bottle with a handmade tag. A subtle food coloring can be added to create appealing shades: green is a popular color for a basil vinegar, red for a chili-pepper vinegar, and yellow for a dill- or garlic-flavored vinegar. Also, the use of certain herbs will naturally color a vinegar. Purple basil, for example, will produce a pink coloration.

Insect Repellents

When so many newspaper headlines tell of the horrors of chemical insecticides, it's no wonder a number of people are turning to earth-friendly herbal solutions. Surprisingly, many of the aromas of herbs that we find pleasant, insects find distinctly unpleasant! Lavender and chamomile are among insect-repelling herbs. They can be rubbed on the skin to repel mosquitoes and gnats or placed in sachets in drawers or closets to deter moths. Garlic and chili peppers are both potent insect repellents that can be planted as companions in flower and vegetable gardens to keep away damaging pests. Indeed, a mixture of garlic and chili peppers, liquefied in a blender and mixed with water, can be used as an effective spray to protect plants from a whole host of chewing insects. Other good herbs to consider for their insect-repelling properties are cedar shavings, lemon thyme, lemongrass, pennyroyal, peppermint, pyrethrum, santolina, southernwood, and tansy.

Potpourri

Before the introduction of air fresheners, herbs, placed in bowls and sprinkled over floors as deodorants, were valued for their use in masking unpleasant household odors. Some herbs, such as rose-scented geraniums and sweet Annie, will deodorize a room by themselves. But the value of a potpourri (a

Colorful potpourris are a wonderful way to introduce a hint of the outdoors to a genteel tabletop vignette. The fragrant dried petals recall days spent out in the garden even when we are snowed in during freezing winters.

mixture of aromatic herbs) comes not just with its rich array of scents, but also with the appealing colors that the mixture can produce, especially when it is arranged in a bowl or stored in glass jars.

A true potpourri is a blend of scented petals and spices. The most successful potpourri blends a mixture of aromatic leaves and seeds, fragrant wood shavings, and fruit peels and flower petals for added color. Particularly important are petals of fragrant roses, carnations, and sweet violets. The ingredients that add fragrance are called blenders. To make potpourri long-lasting, add drops of complementary concentrated oils, such as lavender and rose oil to a blend that features mostly lavender flowers and rose petals.

To keep potpourri fragrant for an extended period, it is important to use a fixative. Traditionally, the favorite fixative has been chunks or flakes of orris root (a flowering plant that looks like a bearded iris) and sweet flag root, a grasslike, bog-loving plant usually sold under the name calamus. Unfortunately, some people have an allergic reaction to orris root, but not to sweet flag or other substitute fixatives. Here at Cedaridge Farm, sweet flag grows wild along a stream, so we have an unlimited supply of it. We simply pull up the rhizomelike roots, cut them into 1-inch (2.5cm) sections, and allow them to air dry. Then we grate these sections more finely using a coarse grater or potato slicer. Synthetic fixatives are available in craft stores, but both orris and sweet flag root add an appealing fragrance of their own.

Whatever fixative you choose, the principles involved in using it are the same. The fixative is combined with concentrated oils, set aside so it fully absorbs the aromas, and then mixed with the other ingredients.

Potpourri

Here's a recipe for a floral-based potpourri that reminds me of the fragrances I encountered in the flower markets of Provence. This recipe makes about ¹⁄₂ gallon of potpourri.

Ingredients

- ³⁄₄ cup of orris root or calamus root chopped into small chunks or flakes
- 1 cup of lavender flowers
- 1 cup of fragrant pink rose petals
- 1 cup of fragrant yellow rose petals
- 1 cup of fragrant red rose buds
- 1 cup rose-scented geranium leaves
- 2 cups chocolate mint leaves
- 1 cup of lemon or orange peel
- 1 cup marigold petals
- 1 cup anise hyssop leaves
- 1 cup rosemary leaves
- ¹⁄₁₆ oz. rose geranium oil
- ¹⁄₁₆ oz. lavender oil
- ¹⁄₁₆ oz. heliotrope oil

Combine the orris or calamus root with the oils of lavender, rose geranium, and heliotrope in a bowl and cover for 2 days. Then combine the mixture with all the other ingredients and store in a glass jar for 3 weeks, stirring once a week to ensure a good blend of aromas and fixative. Then scoop the potpourri into bowls and place them around the house, especially in the bathroom, bedroom, and wherever a pleasant, natural fragrance is desired.

Wreaths and Dried Crafts

There are limitless ways to use herbs in handicrafts such as wreaths. The trick is to retain as much color as possible, and this is a question of proper drying (see "Drying Herbs," page 58). At Cedaridge Farm, my wife, Carolyn, has a special drying room—a converted toolshed—in which she not only dries the herbs, but also has tables and materials with which to make her handicrafts.

The best wreaths demand a combination of flower arranging skills and good drying techniques; once you have the dried ingredients, the wreath is only as successful as the arrangement you make of the colors, textures, and shapes.

Making an Herbal Wreath

The easiest way to make an herbal wreath is to use a preformed frame, made of wire or flexible branches. The frame will have a hollow interior into which you can push dry sphagnum moss. Push the herb stems through the frame and wrap green 18-gauge wire around them for security. As you work, keep checking to make sure that the wreath has a balanced look. The finished dried herbal wreath makes a fragrant and long-lasting decoration for a front door or interior wall, and wreaths and other dried-herb handicrafts are also wonderful to give as gifts.

The Most
Useful Herbs
to Grow

*Opposite: The furry texture and silvery color of lamb's ears combine well
with English lavender's gray-green leaves and dusty purple flowers.*

This encyclopedia of herbs contains those that are most valuable for culinary use, particularly flavoring. Also included is a selection of herbs for other purposes, such as fragrant potpourri, insect repellents, and healing. Since herbs in general can be grown in all hardiness zones as potted plants, both indoors and out, zones of hardiness are not given. In cases where an herb is tender—in need of winter protection or moving indoors during freezing weather—it is noted in the plant's description.

Angelica
(*Angelica archangelica*)

The large flower heads and long stems of angelica add impressive height and structure to herb gardens.

These plants are closely related to parsnips and carrots, and have such a tall, stately presence that they are often used in mixed perennial borders to provide a strong structural and foliage accent. The leaves are like giant celery, composed of many-toothed leaflets arranged in a fan. The hardy perennial plants grow to 5 feet (1.5m) tall, and are topped with branching flower stems and prominent, globular, lime green flower clusters. A long, thick, carrot-like taproot penetrates deep down into the soil.

The leaves and chopped young stems of angelica have a very pleasant, slightly musky flavor, often used in vegetable or seafood soups, salads, and meat sauces. The root is used to make liqueur.

Sow seeds ¼-inch (0.5cm) deep in late summer into a humus-rich, moist soil where the plants are to bloom. Space plants at least 4 feet (1.2m) apart. Angelica plants produce such a long, strong taproot that they are difficult to transplant after their juvenile stage. Although angelica is perennial, it generally exhausts itself after the third or fourth year. Harvest the fresh leaves all summer and the roots in autumn after heavy frost kills the top growth. Harvesting the root (by digging it up) kills the plant, of course. The leaves, chopped stems, and chopped roots can be stored in closed jars.

Anise

(*Pimpinella anisum*)

Anise resembles Queen Anne's lace, or wild carrot. It produces tall, green, feathery stems topped with white flower clusters arranged in an umbrella shape. Anise grows to 2 feet (60cm) tall, and produces whitish seeds in small boat-shaped pods.

Anise is mostly grown for its pungent, licorice-flavored seeds, which are used in baking—particularly to add flavor to sweet rolls and gourmet bread. The crushed seeds also enhance the flavor of desserts such as fresh fruit salads, and they help improve the flavor of mushroom dishes. They are used to produce a licorice-flavored liqueur.

A hardy annual, anise plants must be grown from seeds started indoors 8 weeks before outdoor planting, or direct-seeded several weeks before the last expected frost date in spring. Cover seeds with ¼ inch (0.5cm) of fine soil. Thin seedlings to stand at least 6 inches (15cm) apart. These plants tolerate alkaline soil. The seed heads, or umbels, need

Delicate white anise flowers are followed by brittle brown seed cases filled with aromatic amber seeds. The seeds can be chewed, and have historically been served at the end of a meal to freshen the breath and aid digestion.

a warm, sunny, dry period to ripen properly. When the umbels turn brown and brittle, cut them from the plant and hang upside down over a paper bag, shaking vigorously to loosen the seeds. Store seeds in airtight glass jars or tins.

Anise Hyssop

(Agastache foeniculum)

White and purple flowering varieties of anise hyssop are so beautiful that they look right at home in an ornamental flower garden. A bonus of anise hyssop flowers—they are beloved by both honeybees and hummingbirds.

All parts of the anise hyssop plant have a pleasant anise, or licorice, fragrance reminiscent of root beer. This hardy perennial grows a vigorous clump of erect, poker-straight flower stems topped with mostly lavender-blue, pink, or white flower spikes which are highly attractive to butterflies. Related to mints and possessing the square stems typical of the mint family, anise hyssop grows to 3 feet (90cm) tall, displaying serrated, spear-shaped leaves. The flowers are so ornamental they are often included in mixed perennial borders.

Propagated either by division or from seed, anise hyssop is a sun-loving hardy perennial that will bloom the first year from seed, tolerating a wide range of soil conditions provided drainage is good. Plants readily self-sow, seeding themselves and sprouting in bare soil, but seed also can be started 6 weeks before outdoor planting. Anise hyssop makes a fine container plant, planted one to each gallon container.

The entire plant, including the flowers and the seeds, has a strong anise fragrance and flavor. The dried seeds may be used as a flavoring substitute for regular anise in bakery goods like bread and cookies. Also, the leaves may be brewed to make a refreshing tea. The flower stems may be cut close to the ground and hung to dry so the poker-like flower head turns a rich russet-brown—it's very decorative hung from beams. The crumpled flower head may be added to potpourri and sprinkled on floors to mask unpleasant household smells. A tasty syrup can be made from 5 flower heads of anise by combining them chopped with 1 cup of water and 1 cup of sugar in a pan. Cook over medium heat, stirring until thickened. Simmer for a few minutes and then pour hot over ice cream, or cool over a fruit salad.

Basil

(*O c i m u m   b a s i l i c u m*)

There are many kinds of basil, but the most common culinary herb is sweet basil, a fast-growing tender annual with lustrous, heavily veined, spear-shaped leaves and clusters of small white flowers arranged in a spike. Sweet basil grows to 2 feet (60cm) tall, and flowers in the summer. Its strong, sweet, piquant flavor is frequently used in tomato dishes: a little goes a long way.

Other varieties of basil include 'Green Globe' (it forms a compact, mound-shaped plant like a miniature boxwood); 'Green Ruffles' (a tall, bushy type growing to 4 feet [1.2m] tall, with attractive, ruffled leaves that resemble a coleus); 'Cinnamon' (exhibiting handsome purple stems and conspicuous pink flowers); and 'Thai Lemon Basil' (with a distinct citrus flavor).

There are also several bronze or purple-leaf basils, including 'Purple Ruffles' and 'Dark Opal'. The latter two are more often seen in flower gardens than herb gardens, because their flavor is not so strong as the green basils. They create striking background contrasts for brightly colored annuals.

Basils are tender annuals best grown from seed started indoors, planted ¼-inch (0.5cm) deep, 6 to 8 weeks before outdoor planting. The seed needs warmth (70°F [21°C]) to germinate. Once sprouted, the seedlings should be watered sparingly to prevent rot.

Cinnamon basil has purple stems, pink flowers, and bronze leaves, and looks especially distinguished set off from the garden in decorative pots.

Cuttings also root readily in water. A good way to ensure a continuous supply of basil all season is to take cuttings from mature plants in midsummer for transplanting back into the garden as soon as a healthy set of roots has emerged.

Spring-planted basil generally loses vigor before the end of summer, and a second planting for autumn harvest is advisable. Space plants at least 12 inches (30cm) apart. A sandy or well-drained loam soil is best; site the plants in full sun.

The fresh leaves are good to chop fine and sprinkle over sliced raw tomatoes and in salads. Also use them sprinkled in tomato sauce and over pizza. Chopped basil is the key ingredient in pesto. It is also used to flavor vegetable soups, ratatouille, omelettes, and fish chowders. Harvest the top whorl of leaves, then chop and freeze the leaves to store them. Freezing turns the leaves black, but does not affect the flavor. Basil also makes a flavorful vinegar. 'Thai Lemon Basil' (*Ocimum basilicum citriodorum*) is a valuable ingredient for Thai dishes involving rice, fish, and poultry.

Bay is a long-lived woody plant that is most successfully grown in containers in regions that experience freezing winters. The containers can be moved indoors in winter to protect the tender plants.

Bay

(*Laurus nobilis*)

Bay is a somewhat tender, evergreen woody plant. Its leaves are smooth, lustrous, leathery, and spear-shaped. In ancient Greek and Roman times, the leaves were used to create garlands and crowns symbolizing heroic stature. The plants grow as bushy shrubs or small trees. Where winters are severe, they are usually confined to planter boxes so they can be moved indoors when cold weather arrives. The leaves have a strong, spicy aroma and fragrance.

Bay plants prefer a humus-rich, fertile soil and full sun, and should be spaced at least 3 feet (90cm) apart. They are propagated mostly from cuttings.

Although they are slow-growing, the plants can be pruned into topiary forms (such as balls and pyramids) by severe pruning, or they may be trained to produce a single straight trunk with a topknot of leaves. Planted in Versailles-style planter boxes, they are often used as accents in formal herb gardens.

The brittle leaves can be snapped in two and the vapor released will clear a congested nose. The aroma and flavor intensify upon drying. The dried leaves are used to flavor vegetable soups and meat stews; one leaf is usually sufficient to flavor 1 gallon (3.7L) of soup. Dried leaves can be stored for several years in tins. The fresh and dried leaves are popular components of herbal wreaths.

Bee Balm
(*Monarda didyma*)

Bee balm is not only highly attractive to bees, it is a virtual magnet for butterflies and hummingbirds as well.

Native to North America, bee balm (also known as bergamot) is an aggressive, clump-forming, hardy perennial plant closely related to mint, with square stems and serrated, spear-shaped, gray-green leaves that have a musky odor and smoky flavor when brewed into a tea. In the summer the plants are topped with crowns of conspicuous red, pink, purple, or white clusters of tubular florets. These flowers are highly attractive to hummingbirds. Plants grow to 4 feet (1.2m) tall, and are often included in mixed perennial borders.

Bee balm prefers full sun and good drainage, but otherwise tolerates poor soil. It is propagated mostly by division, but some interesting colors can be obtained by growing plants from seed. Plants will flower the second season when started from seed. Several seed mixtures are sold by mail-order companies. When sowing seed, plant ¼ inch (0.5cm) deep. If starting indoors, transplant from gallon (3.7L) containers, spacing plants at least 3 feet (90cm) apart.

The leaves make a refreshing hot tea, and can be brewed either freshly picked or dried. The flavor is more pronounced after drying. Store the dried leaves in screw-top jars or tins.

Borage is one of the most profuse flowering herbs, blooming nonstop from midsummer to autumn frost.

Borage
(*Borago officinalis*)

This bushy tender annual grows to 3 feet (90cm) tall. It has hairy, spear-shaped green leaves, and produces loose clusters of smoky blue, star-shaped flowers that are highly attractive to bees.

Sow seed directly into the garden in a sunny position after danger of frost, or start seed indoors 6 weeks earlier, sowing the seed ¼ inch (0.5cm) deep. Space plants at least 2 feet (60cm) apart and water regularly. Borage makes an attractive pot plant in a gallon size (3.7L) or larger container. These plants self-seed readily.

The young fresh leaves have a cucumber flavor that is pleasant mixed into salads or added to a glass of white wine. Borage flowers are edible and are also highly decorative; they're a favorite ingredient in salads using other floral ingredients like nasturtiums and viola petals. The leaves do not store well.

Burnet
(*Sanguisorba major*)

Burnet forms low-spreading clumps of toothed oval leaves on long, arching stems. The small red flowers are held erect in early summer. It is especially beautiful used as an edging to paths.

Although burnet is a hardy perennial and propagation by division is possible, the plants become weak after flowering in the second season. The best results are always

Right: The leaves of burnet are arranged in a fishbone pattern. It is an excellent low-growing plant for edging beds and borders. Below: Though caraway blooms are not long-lasting, they make an impact in the garden with their clouds of attractive lacy white flowers.

achieved by starting this herb from seed, sowing in spring ¼ inch (0.5cm) deep into a well-drained soil in a sunny position. Thin seedlings to stand at least 12 inches apart. Or, start seeds 8 weeks before outdoor planting. The plants will readily self-sow.

The leaves have a flavor reminiscent of cucumber. They are used fresh chopped into salads, egg dishes, and herbal sauces. Burnet leaves turn tough and lose their flavor when dried.

Caraway
(*Carum carvi*)

These plants resemble wild carrot, with feathery leaves and erect stems topped by clusters of small white flowers arranged in a lacy umbrella. Caraway is a biennial that dies after flowering, but it will self-seed readily.

Sow seeds in spring or late summer directly into the garden in a sunny, well-drained spot. Cover with just enough soil to anchor the seeds, since they prefer light to germinate.

Caraway plants form parsleylike clumps the first year, followed by tall, spindly seed heads the second. They tolerate crowding, but ideally should stand at least 6 inches (15cm) apart so they have space to thrive.

The ripe seeds and young leaves have a sweet, aromatic flavor that is especially tasty when added to boiled cabbage, potatoes, and cottage cheese. Harvest the seed when the pods turn brown and brittle and store them in a screw-top jar. The leaves do not store well, though the seeds do.

Catmint and Catnip
(*Nepeta mussinii* and *Nepeta cataria*)

Both *Nepeta mussinii* and *Nepeta × faassenii* (a hybrid) are attractive ornamental perennial plants known as catmints. Their flowers are a gorgeous blue, though the hybrid is more free-flowering than the regular species. They are often confused with *Nepeta cataria* (catnip), which is a rather coarse, unattractive plant.

The leaves of both catmint and catnip are similar—a gray-green color, serrated and spear-shaped, but the resemblance ends there. Catnip has inconspicuous, small white flowers and it will grow to 3 feet (90cm) tall, twice the height of the other two species. Catnip has one amazing property that catmints usually lack—a slight musky, minty fragrance that sends cats

Catnip is named and best known for its powerful attraction to felines, who will roll on plants set out in the garden. This plant is also thought to repel rats and insects.

into fits of ecstasy. Sniff catnip yourself and you'll wonder what it is that cats like about it, since the aroma is so slight. The catmints are more fragrant to human noses, but the leaves of both can be brewed to make a refreshing tea.

Start these two species from seeds or propagate by division, planting outdoors in spring or late summer and early autumn. Seeds can be direct-sown and lightly covered with soil or started indoors 8 weeks before outdoor planting. Plant nepeta in full sun in a well-drained soil. Space plants at least 3 feet (90cm) apart.

Although both catnip and catmint are used for herbal teas, they tend to be an acquired taste. Their most popular use by far is for pleasing cats. Grown in pots on a sunny windowsill, the leaves can be picked fresh and placed into a sock for cats to play with. Outdoors, cats will literally swoon over catnip, pressing their cheeks and noses against the leaves and rolling in it joyfully.

Chamomile
(*Matricaria recutita*)

There is much confusion about chamomile, since there are many daisylike plants that look alike and have a chamomile fragrance to the leaves. Some are perennial, but *M. recutita*, the most commonly grown, is a hardy annual that grows feathery, gray-green foliage and covers itself in white daisylike flowers with yellow button centers. The plants grow to 1½ feet (45.5cm) tall, in a perfect dome shape. Real chamomile has a light apple fragrance, while chamomile look-alikes have either no discernible fragrance or a sharp, unpleasant aroma.

Chamomile's reputation for calming frayed nerves has made it a favorite ingredient in herbal teas.

Sow seeds in the spring or autumn, covering with just enough soil to anchor the seed, in a sunny site with good drainage. Although chamomile plants tolerate crowding, they are best spaced at least 6 inches (15cm) apart.

The leaves are used fresh or dried, mostly in a soothing, refreshing tea and as an aid to digestion. The dried leaves are more intensely flavored than the fresh leaves. Air-dried chamomile blossoms are also valued for adding to potpourri, as an insect repellent in sachets to repel moths, or rubbed on the skin to repel gnats.

A favorite of French cooks, chervil is one of the *fines herbes.* Chervil fares well planted in a pot or in a sunny window box, so you can have it on hand even if your garden space is relatively small.

Chervil
(*Anthriscus cerefolium*)

This hardy annual produces clumps of soft, feathery leaves on erect stems topped by flat, white flower clusters. The finely cut foliage has a smooth, spicy, aniselike flavor.

Plant chervil seeds outdoors in spring several weeks before the last frost date, or in autumn. This herb does best direct-seeded into a sunny, well-drained location. Cover the seed just enough to anchor it. The plants will tolerate crowding, but they are best spaced at least 6 inches (15cm) apart. Make succession sowings every 3 to 4 weeks to ensure a continuous supply of fresh leaves.

Harvest the young leaves until the plants go to seed, using them like parsley to flavor soups, sauces, salads, and egg dishes. Use fresh leaves only, as they do not store well.

Chili Peppers
(*Capsicum annuum*)

Chili peppers are not only the source of hot chili flavor, but the fruits of its many varieties are also highly ornamental. The bushy 3- to 4-foot (90 to 120cm) tall plants have dark green, smooth, spear-shaped leaves and round, cone-shaped, or tapered fruits, which usually change from green to red when ripe. The degree of hotness can also vary among varieties. Both the fruits and the seeds are useful as a garnish.

Chili peppers are particularly useful in the herb garden for the spot of bright red color the fruits contribute, a hue not found in many other herbs.

These tender hardy annuals are best grown from seeds started indoors 8 weeks before outdoor planting. Sow the seeds ¼ inch (0.5cm) deep. Chili peppers relish a warm, fertile soil in a sunny location. A mulch of black plastic over the soil encourages the earliest, heaviest yields. Chili peppers are attractive grown in containers of at least 1 gallon (3.7L). Some varieties have a spreading habit and are suitable for hanging baskets. In the garden, space plants at least 2 feet (60cm) apart.

The fruits are generally harvested when they are red. The branches can be cut from the plant and hung to dry with the peppers attached. The fruits are then chopped fine and stored in airtight containers for sprinkling over any foods requiring a spicy, hot flavor—egg dishes, curries, chili, stews, tomato sauces, and pizzas. The 'Cayenne' variety of chili pepper is also useful at Thanksgiving and Christmas to make decorative dried wreaths. The fruits are a favorite ingredient in herbal vinegar, and the dried seeds may be stored in jars to use as a garnish for sprinkling over pizza. The fruits of chili peppers can be steeped in water to make a liquid spray for repelling insect pests and rodents in flower and vegetable gardens.

Chives

(*Allium schoenoprasum*)

A valued companion planting for roses and other pest-bedeviled plants, chives discourage aphids and Japanese beetles, among other insects.

This hardy perennial grows in compact clumps of spiky, round, hollow, onion-flavored green leaves up to 12 inches (30cm) tall. In late spring, chives produce masses of beautiful rounded pink flowers. Chives are so ornamental that they are often included in mixed perennial borders as an edging.

Chives can be propagated by seeds and by division of the bulb clusters; they self-seed readily. When growing from seed either direct-sow ¼ inch (0.5cm) deep where plants are to bloom several weeks before the last frost date, or start indoors by sowing thinly into a seed starting tray. When the seedlings reach 4 inches (10cm) they can be transplanted into the garden. The bulbs can be separated at any time and transplanted, though this is usually done in the autumn. Plants prefer spacing at least 6 inches (15cm) apart and demand a sunny position to flower. Chives make excellent container plants, even growing contentedly in coffee cans on a kitchen window sill.

The leaves are chopped fine and used to flavor soups, potatoes, cottage cheese, herbal sauces, salads, or wherever an onion flavor is desired. The flower heads also have an onion flavor, and are used as a decoration at buffet tables, floated in meat sauces. These plants can be harvested continuously. The chopped leaves store best when frozen.

Coriander
(*Coriandrum sativum*)

Also called cilantro and Chinese parsley, this hardy annual grows feathery, sweetly flavored leaves on erect stems topped by clusters of white flowers that resemble Queen Anne's lace. The plants grow to 3 feet (90cm) tall. The seeds, which are formed in umbrellalike pods, are also aromatic.

Sow seeds directly into the garden several weeks before the last frost date, covering with just enough soil to anchor them. Although these plants can tolerate crowding, the seedlings are best thinned to stand at least 12 inches (30cm) apart. Give them full sun and good drainage.

The fresh leaves are used to flavor roasted peppers and fried tomatoes; they can also be sprinkled into stir-fry dishes. The seeds are used in gingerbread. For a good flavor in the seeds, allow the seed stalk to turn brittle, and then shuck the dried seeds into a bag. Store them in a screw-top jar. The leaves do not store well.

Coriander was one of the earliest cultivated spices, and is still used extensively in many of the world's cuisines.

Curry Plant
(*Helichrysum angustifolium*)

A somewhat tender perennial in Zones 6 north, curry plant can be grown as an annual where winters are severe or in containers that will be moved indoors during winter. The bushy plants grow to 2 feet (60cm) tall, with aromatic, silvery, narrow, needlelike leaves. Small, yellow buttonlike flowers are produced on erect stems in the late summer.

Above: While curry plant is not a substitute for the hot Indian spice, it does impart a delicate curry flavor to dishes. Below: Dill is a favorite in herb gardens for its contributions both ornamental and culinary.

Propagate from seeds or tip cuttings. Start seeds indoors 8 weeks before outdoor planting, covering the seeds with just a light layer of soil. These plants require full sun and good drainage, and tolerate hot, dry conditions. Space them at least 2 feet (60cm) apart.

Curry plant is used as a seasoning for salads, egg dishes, and stews. It is not a replacement for the specially formulated curry powders used in hot Indian curries, but its pleasant curry flavor and aroma are unmistakable. Most of the ingredients for Indian curry are tender perennials that are difficult to grow in North American gardens.

Dill

(A n e t h u m   g r a v e o l e n s)

Dill is a tall annual, which can grow to 4 feet (1.2m). It has fine, gray-green, feathery foliage on erect stems topped by umbels of yellow flower clusters. All parts of the plant, including the seeds, are aromatic and useful as a flavoring. The variety 'Fern-leaf' is unusually floriferous and not as tall-growing. It can be grown for ornamental effect.

Dill is easily grown from seed sown ¼ inch (0.5cm) deep, directly into the garden. In fact, it is one of the most aggressive self-seeders of all herb varieties. Once you have a clump established in your garden, all you have to do is cultivate the volunteer seedlings that spring up around the previous year's planting. Plants tolerate crowding, but are best thinned to 6 inches (15cm) apart. Make succession sowings every 4 weeks to ensure a continuous supply.

The leaves are used fresh, chopped fine to flavor seafood, salads, and egg dishes. They are particularly tasty sprinkled over cucumbers, sliced tomatoes, and potatoes. The seeds are a flavor enhancer when added to vinegar in pickling and are best stored in airtight containers. The leaves may be stored dried or frozen.

Fennel

(*Foeniculum vulgare*)

Fast-growing annual fennel likes cool weather to develop its crisp, flavorful bulbous base.

Fennel is a tender annual with straight, succulent, oval stems which sprout from a bulbous root sheath. Feathery green or bronze leaves arch out along the stems. The plants grow to 4 feet (1.2m) tall, and produce yellow or brownish flower clusters arranged in an umbel. The aromatic seeds have an anise flavor.

This herb is best grown from seeds either direct-sown ¼ inch (0.5cm) deep, or started indoors 6 weeks before outdoor planting. Transplant several weeks before the last frost date, since plants can tolerate light frosts and need cool conditions to grow well. Make a second sowing in late summer for an autumn harvest of this useful herb.

The bulbous root sheath is crisp and edible, and is often sliced into salads. It is considered by many to be a gourmet delicacy. The roots are best if the plants are grown in a fertile, humus-rich soil in full sun, and watered regularly. The leaves may be chopped fine to add an anise-like flavor to salads and sauces. The seeds may also be used for flavoring.

Garlic

(*Allium sativum*)

Garlic is closely related to onions, and in fact, resembles its cousin. Plants grow slender, wavy, smooth blue-green leaves and a cone-shaped, white flower cluster that matures into small brown bulblets in a pointed sheath. Below ground, the plant grows a white, onionlike bulb with a papery sheath that encloses edible segments called cloves.

Although garlic is a hardy perennial, it is best grown as an annual from cloves that should be planted into the garden in late summer or early autumn of the year prior to harvesting. Plant them so that the pointed segments of the cloves are just below the soil surface. The cloves can immediately sprout leaves, survive even harsh winters, and produce large edible bulbs by midsummer. Give them full sun, and a fertile, well-drained, humus-rich soil.

All parts of the plant have a sharp, pungent onion flavor which is at its most concentrated form in the underground

Garlic is best planted in autumn and harvested the following summer. Once the bulbs have been dug from the ground, hang them up to dry.

bulb. The chopped bulbs are useful as a flavor enhancer in almost all cooked dishes, but especially those of Mediterranean and Asian origin, such as stir-fry, pasta, and rice pilaf. The size and pungency of the bulb change according to variety; for example, 'Elephant' garlic is mild and will grow to the size of an orange.

The bulbs can be dried for storage and hung with their dried stems braided into decorative garlic ropes. The cloves may also be steeped in vinegar and oil to create a useful garlic-flavored condiment. Also, the bulbs can be squeezed and mixed with water to create a potent insect repellent spray for the flower and vegetable garden.

Garlic Chives

(Allium tuberosum)

The leaves of garlic chives have a mild garlic flavor. White flower clusters, appearing in late summer, are a handsome bonus.

These hardy perennial bulbs are almost evergreen, similar in appearance to regular chives, but with a flattened leaf blade. Garlic chives form taller clumps (to 2 feet [60cm]), and in summer produce star-shaped white flowers clustered in wide, flat umbels. The leaves have a mild garlic flavor and push through the soil at the slightest hint of a warming trend in early spring.

Garlic chives are easily propagated by division of established clumps; each bulblet produces a new plant. The black seeds also germinate readily either direct-sown ¼ inch (0.5cm) deep or started indoors 8 weeks before outdoor planting. They tolerate a wide range of soils provided drainage is good and the site is sunny.

Garlic chives are an excellent salad ingredient to mix with lettuce, endive, spinach, and other salad greens. Use them chopped into egg dishes and wherever a mild garlic

Scented-leaf geraniums are excellent for potted gardens or for edging paths, where the leaves will be brushed against, releasing their fragrance.

flavor is desired, such as over pizza, in stews, soups, cottage cheese, and in herbal sauces. Store chopped leaves by freezing them for the 2 or 3 months during winter when you will not be able to harvest the leaves fresh.

Geraniums, Scented-Leaf

(*Pelargonium graveolens* and other species)

There are many kinds of scented-leaf geraniums, most of which are native to South Africa. The most popular is the rose-scented geranium, but there are also lemon-scented, nutmeg-scented, pineapple-scented, and other varieties. Most scented geraniums produce a bushy growth habit up to several feet tall. Not only are the leaves different shapes, colors, and textures, but they can have vastly different flowers (though the flowers are usually sparse, in white and shades of pink). The predominant leaf type is ivy-shaped, and often the leaves have a velvety or woolly texture. To capitalize on their fragrance, group several different varieties of scented-leaf geraniums around a bench, for the mere action of the sun shining on a leaf, or the slightest touch, will release their aromas into the atmosphere.

Scented-leaf geraniums are best propagated by tip cuttings (see pages 30-31 for instructions) or from rooted cuttings purchased from a mail-order houseplant nursery. They are all tender perennials, surviving winters only in frost-free areas. However, all of these plants are suitable for container growing. When frost threatens, simply dig up a clump, prune its stems back to the soil line, and overwinter it indoors. New sprouts will appear during winter, and when transferred to the garden after danger of frost, the plants will fill out and grow bushy again.

Scented-leaf geraniums are an important component of fragrance gardens and of potpourri. The lemon- and rose-scented kinds are grown commercially to provide fragrances for soaps and perfumes. A useful technique is to insert a rose- or lemon-scented geranium leaf into the bottom of a cookie mold so that when the mold is removed from the oven the baked leaf has made a decorative imprint on the underside of the cookie, as well as imparting its distinctive flavor.

Germander

(*Teucrium chamaedrys*)

A hardy, woody perennial, germander grows a dense weave of branches and glossy, spear-shaped leaves. Small pink flowers appear in the summer. These plants are evergreen in mild winter areas. There is a handsome silvery tender species, *T. majoricum*, that grows to 5 feet (1.5m) tall in frost-free areas, and can be used as a decorative hedge.

Germander is usually grown from cuttings taken after flowering and held over the winter in cold frames to produce transplants for the following spring. The plants prefer full sun and good drainage. For a hedge effect, space plants 12 inches (30cm) apart.

Its primary use is in creating parterres and knot gardens, since the plants tolerate heavy pruning. The fresh stems and perky pink flowers are used in herbal wreaths and potpourri. They can be dried by hanging upside down in bunches.

Hardy, evergreen germander can be used as a decorative groundcover or as an edging plant. It also looks great planted in rock walls or between paving stones.

Ginseng

(*Panax quinquefolius*) This elusive North American woodland wildflower grows mostly in the Appalachian Mountains, thriving in light to deep shade in well-drained, humus-rich, acidic soil. The plants grow clusters of serrated, pointed leaves that are arranged in a fan like a chestnut leaf. They emerge in the spring from a fleshy root that resembles a forked parsnip. Ginseng plants grow to 2 feet (60cm) tall, and produce inconspicuous greenish white flowers that turn into bright red berries.

They can be propagated by seeds, but be aware that the seeds germinate erratically and can take up to 2 years to sprout. For quicker results, start from young roots purchased by mail. Plant at least 3 feet (90cm) apart and never allow the soil to dry out. When growing ginseng from seed, it is best to create a special nursery bed in a lightly shaded area, with boards used to raise the soil at least 12 inches (30cm) above the existing soil level. Sprinkle the seed lightly, and cover with just enough soil to anchor it.

Keep the nursery bed cool and moist. Seedlings can take up to 7 years to reach full maturity.

Ginseng has been listed as a threatened species, and should never be taken from the wild. Its roots, which are used both fresh and dried, have a variety of culinary and medicinal purposes.

The ginseng root is grated into a powder and dried to make an invigorating herbal tea. A pinch of powder in a teacup makes an energy-restoring hot drink. Slivers of the root may also be eaten raw. Ginseng is much valued in Asia, where it is considered an aphrodisiac and cure-all for a variety of illnesses, mostly to do with colds, heartburn, and depression. Beware of "get-rich-quick" schemes involving ginseng: entrepreneurs claim ginseng is so highly prized in China that you can earn big money growing a commercial crop and selling it to exporters. Unfortunately, the average home garden cannot provide the conditions for a large commercial crop, with its need for shade, deep humus-rich soil, wide spacing, and constant watering. A small colony in a cool, shady corner of your garden is the best most gardeners can hope to achieve.

Hops
(*Humulus lupulus, H. japonicus*)

European hops are most widely used in the brewing of beer, with the largest areas of production concentrated in Oregon and New Zealand.

There are two kinds of hops commonly used in herb gardens; both are vigorous vines that need a strong arbor or trellis for support, and must be trained to climb. The two types are the European hop (*H. lupulus*) and the Japanese hop (*H. japonicus*). Both are hardy perennials, though the European hop is more hardy than the Japanese. They have grapelike foliage and clusters of unusual, papery green fruits, called bitters, that are the source of a flavoring for beer. There are some variegated forms of hops available, notably 'Aureus', a European hop with gold leaves.

The Japanese hop, though tender above Zone 7, grows quickly from seed and will top a 12-foot (3.6m) pole or trellis in a single season. The European hop is much hardier (to Zone 5) and it is best propagated from root cuttings. Space the plants at least 4 feet (1.2m) apart in full sun. The soil must have good drainage.

The bitters are an important flavor ingredient in beer, though some modern beers have replaced the real thing with chemical substitutes. The papery fruits are decorative when dried, and are used in herbal wreaths.

Horehound
(*Marrubium vulgare*)

Horehound has a decorative leaf—curled and silvery—making it a good accent in the herb garden. It does well in hot spots, where many other herbs will suffer.

This herb resembles mint, but has a dusky, gray-green leaf and a camphorlike aroma. It's not a particularly attractive plant, growing loose clumps of 3-foot (90cm) - tall stems topped with inconspicuous white flowers. False horehound (*Ballota acetabulosa*) and other *Ballota* species are sometimes used as substitutes for horehound, but true horehound is preferred for making the natural candy recipe given below.

Horehound is usually propagated by cuttings and division. The plants prefer full sun and good drainage; space them at least 3 feet (90cm) apart. Because of its bushy habit, one plant is sufficient for any garden, and you may prefer to grow horehound in a container of at least 1 gallon (3.7L) capacity.

The most common use for horehound is to flavor hard candy, a popular winter confection because it helps to soothe sore throats and relieve colds. To prepare horehound candy place 2 cups of fresh horehound leaves and flowers together in a pot, cover with water and bring to a boil. Simmer for 10 minutes and strain the aromatic liquid through a cheesecloth. Ladle 2 cups of this strained liquid into a kettle. Add 3 cups of brown sugar, ½ cup of corn syrup, and 1 teaspoon of cream of tartar. Boil and stir until the temperature reaches 240°F (115°C). Then add a teaspoon of butter. Continue to boil until the temperature of the mixture reaches 300°F (149°C). Remove from the heat and add 1 teaspoon of lemon juice. Pour the syrupy liquid into a buttered 8-inch (20.5cm) square pan, and as it hardens cut into bite-size squares. Remove from the pan and store in jars or freezer bags.

Horseradish

(*Armoracia rusticana*)

Horseradish is a hardy perennial; its 3-foot (90cm) -tall stems grow wavy, broad, dark green, pointed leaves with small, inconspicuous white flowers. Though horseradish is usually grown as a root crop in sandy soil (to accommodate its long, thick taproot), it is one of a small group of herbs that will grow contentedly with its roots permanently submerged in shallow water. At Cedaridge Farm, we use clumps of horseradish as ornamental waterside plants in our stream garden. The roots are thick, yellow-skinned, and pungent. When peeled, the white pith can be shredded and combined with vinegar to make a mustardlike hot condiment.

Horseradish is usually propagated from sections of root containing a growing point. Since the main idea is to grow a shapely, parsniplike root, the soil should be sandy to a depth of 2 feet (60cm), fertile, and humus-rich, in full sun. Space the plants at least 2 feet (60cm) apart. Divide roots in spring or late summer and early autumn.

As mentioned above, the white, sharp-flavored part of the root can be grated and mixed with vinegar to produce a flavorful garnish for all kinds of meat dishes. To store, pack the paste-vinegar mixture in jars and use it sparingly, as you would hot mustard.

Above: Horseradish grows a long, thick, carrot-shaped taproot. It needs a deep, sandy, fertile soil and regular amounts of water to do well. Below: Because of its dense growth pattern, hyssop has traditionally been planted and pruned in herbal knot gardens.

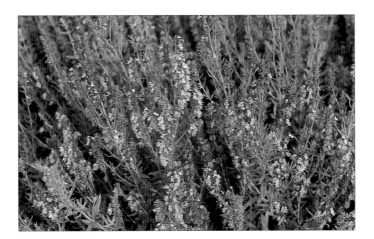

Hyssop

(*Hyssopus officinalis*)

This lavenderlike, bushy, hardy perennial plant grows to 2 feet (60cm) tall. The leaves are narrow, sharp, and pungent like mint; the lavender-blue flowers appear in midsummer.

Hyssop can be propagated from seeds, cuttings, and division. Start seeds

indoors 6 weeks before outdoor planting, sowing them just below the soil surface
Transplant the seedlings to a sunny spot with well-drained soil after danger of severe
frost has passed; space the plants at least 2 feet (60cm) apart.

The fresh leaves can be used as a seasoning for salads, soups, stews, and bean dishes.
Young shoots may be dried and quickly sealed in screw-top jars for storage.

Lavender, English

(*Lavandula angustifolia*)

This beautiful, cushion-shaped plant grows to 3 feet (90cm) high, and spreads twice as wide. Its gray-green leaves resemble pine needles, and its lovely blue or purple fragrant flowers are carried in spiky clusters and bloom all summer. There is perhaps no fragrance in the world more admired than that of lavender. For thousands of years the center for lavender production was the south of England and Provence, but production there has been shrinking rapidly because other areas can grow it more economically. Today, lavender for perfumes and soaps is more likely to be grown in Tasmania, Spain, or Morocco. Though perennial, plants tend to fall apart after several years of blooming.

Lavender demands full sun and excellent drainage. Indeed, its liking for sharp drainage is so great that in clay-soil areas, it is best to create a special raised bed filled with gravel, or to grow these plants along terraces, which tend to drain well.

Lavender makes a beautiful low hedge. In a classic pairing, a lush planting of English lavender defines a rose border.

Propagation is most successfully done from stem cuttings taken in spring and rooted in pots filled with a moist, sandy potting soil. There is one variety of English lavender, 'Lavender Lady', which will grow from seed to flower the first year as an annual. Otherwise, lavender germinates erratically from seed. Prune established lavender plants by simply shaping the plants into a dome in autumn or spring.

In addition to scenting perfumes and soaps, sprigs of lavender (including the flowers) can be used to make a refreshing tea. They also have insect-repellent properties and are good for keeping linen closets clear of moths. Add a few sprigs to bathwater for a pleasant aroma or use the dried stems in potpourri and scented sachets.

Lavender Cotton

(*Santolina chamaecyparissus*)

Lavender cotton produces a beautiful mound of buttonlike yellow flowers. It can also be pruned hard to create a low hedge or herbal knot pattern.

Lavender cotton grows into silvery mounds that reach up to 2 feet (60cm) in height. Its tightly packed, finely indented, aromatic leaves resemble a dwarf evergreen cypress. There is a green-leaf species (*S. virens*), which is often combined with the silver form to create contrasting hedges in herbal knot gardens. In midsummer, plants of both species are covered in yellow buttonlike flowers.

These reasonably hardy perennials are best propagated from cuttings and division. They tolerate dry conditions, and demand a sunny, well-drained position. For hedging

effects, space plants 12 inches (30cm) apart. At the end of each growing season the plants should be pruned to maintain a low-mounded shape. Both forms take heavy pruning to create low hedges for parterres and knot gardens.

The lavender-scented leaves and yellow flowers are used dried in potpourri. The leaves of the silver form are especially valued for herbal wreaths.

Lemon Balm

(*Melissa officinalis*)

Lemon balm has inconspicuous white flowers, but its lemony, mintlike leaves are highly ornamental. It looks best paired with foliage of deep green, and is a well-known attractant for bees.

Related to mint, this bushy hardy perennial grows to 2 feet (60cm) tall, and produces serrated, oval, lemon-flavored leaves and inconspicuous white flowers that bloom in midsummer on erect, square stems.

Lemon balm readily self-seeds. The plants may be divided every 2 years to prevent their spreading aggressively. This herb prefers full sun, tolerates poor soil, and enjoys good drainage. Space the plants at least 2 feet (60cm) apart.

The bittersweet lemon-flavored leaves are tasty chopped and added to salads, herbal sauces, and tomato dishes. The leaves may also be brewed to make a delicious, refreshing tea. Store the leaves dried in screw-top jars.

Lemongrass
(*Cymbopogon citratus*)

This tender perennial grass from India has a decorative, fountainlike habit: its long, slender, arching bright green leaves glow yellow when backlit from the sun. It makes a beautiful accent in the landscape, with just one plant growing to 4 feet (1.2m) tall. It is at its very best when displayed in a decorative container such as an urn. The leaves impart a lemon aroma when picked; the more the leaves are picked, the more leaves are produced.

Lemongrass is best propagated by division. A healthy clump can be separated into dozens of juveniles, each with a tuft of leaves. Plant this herb outdoors only after the danger of frost has passed. These plants grow quickly in bright light during warm weather, and tolerate heat and poor soil provided the drainage is good. Space plants at least 3 feet (90cm) apart. In frost-prone areas, pot plants and overwinter indoors.

The tangy flavor of lemongrass is not only a good substitute for lemons to flavor fish, rice, curry, and other Asian dishes, it is also a natural insect repellent when rubbed on the skin. Lemongrass, rather than real lemons, is usually the favored ingredient in lemon-scented soaps and perfumes. To flavor liquids like iced tea, chop leaves into small segments and use as an infusion (enclose the leaves in a muslin pouch and steep for several minutes). The flavor is best in freshly harvested leaves.

A true grass, native to India, lemongrass produces beautiful, slender, arching leaves that can be chopped fine as a flavoring.

Lovage
(*Levisticum officinale*)

This hardy plant resembles a large specimen of celery. It has strong, erect leaf stalks up to 5 feet (1.5m) tall and sharply indented, aromatic leaves. Yellow flowers bloom in midsummer, clustered in flat umbels.

Lovage is usually grown from seed sown directly into the garden several weeks before the last frost date. Or, seed can be started indoors 6 to 8 weeks before outdoor planting. Sow seeds ¼ inch (0.5cm) deep. Choose a sunny position with well-drained, humus-rich, fertile soil. Space the plants at least 3 feet (90cm) apart.

The leaves have a spicy, celerylike flavor, good for seasoning soups, stews, meat dishes, and salads. The leaves can be dried and stored in screw-top jars.

Marigolds
(*Tagetes* species)

Most marigolds in the wild have spicy-scented, serrated leaves, and daisylike flowers, but modern plant breeding has produced a number of varieties with globe-shaped flowers.

Marigolds can flower so prolifically that the flowers will almost completely hide the foliage, making them favorite plants for flower gardens. This is especially true of the bushy, compact, mound-shaped plants of French marigolds (*T. patula*), and the more diminutive signet marigolds (*T. tenuifolia*). These grow to 12 inches (30cm) tall, but the large-flowered African marigolds (*T. erecta*) can reach 3 feet (90cm) tall. Because the leaves have a strong, unpleasant flavor, few gardeners realize that the petals of

Above: Lovage resembles a giant celery plant, and has a similar flavor as well. Below: 'Gem' marigolds make a decorative edging along a gravel path.

marigolds are edible; the orange-petaled varieties, in particular, can make an acceptable substitute for the costliest of all spices—saffron. There is also a tender perennial marigold, *T. lucida*, which has a licorice aroma reminiscent of root beer. *T. lucida* grows 2 feet (60cm) tall.

All annual marigolds grow easily from seed sown directly into the garden after danger of frost, and thinned to stand at least 12 inches (30cm) apart. The soil should be well drained and in full sun, but not overly fertile since this can produce more leaves than flowers. For earliest blooms, start seed indoors 6 to 8 weeks before outdoor planting, sown ¼ inch (0.5cm) deep. If the faded flowers are removed, marigolds will continue blooming all summer until autumn frosts. The perennial marigold can be propagated from tip cuttings or division. Dwarf, compact varieties are especially suitable for growing in containers.

Sprinkle marigold petals over salads to add color, or use them as an economical substitute for saffron. The perennial marigold can be used as a substitute for tarragon. Its leaves are brittle when dry and are good to add to potpourri. The African marigold (*Tagetes erecta*) has particularly good pest-repellent properties, and helps to control flea beetle and nematode infestations.

Different marjoram cultivars vary in their flowering performance. Several varieties are now available with deep pink flower heads like these.

Marjoram
(*Origanum majorana*)

There is much confusion between the herbs marjoram and oregano since they are similar species and look alike. However, the true sweet marjoram has the best flavor and it is the variety most often used to flavor meals. These mound-shaped perennial plants grow just 12 inches (30cm) tall, and have glossy, pointed leaves that have a spicy taste and scent. The plants are covered in summer with beautiful clusters of white or pink flowers. Plants are tender and do not survive severe winters.

Except in frost-free locations, sweet marjoram is best grown as an annual, started from seed indoors 6 weeks before outdoor planting. Sow the seeds just below the soil surface. Marjoram tolerates poor soil, and prefers full sun and good drainage. Space the plants at least 12 inches (30cm) apart.

Marjoram is a favorite flavor enhancer for many kinds of meat dishes and soups, as well as herbal sauces and pizza. When dried, the leaves may be stored in screw-top jars.

Medicine Plant

(Aloe vera, A. barbadensis)

Aloe vera is a tender succulent plant native to the deserts of Africa. It has spiny, pointed, gray-green leaves and spires of yellowish-orange, trumpet-shaped flowers that appear in early spring. The leaves have a leathery skin, but their interior is filled with a light green gel that is moist and soothing to the touch.

Medicine plants not only make good houseplants, they will grow on dry slopes in frost-free areas.

These perennial plants are highly sensitive to frost, and any prolonged temperatures below 50°F (10°C) will subject them to stress. Medicine plant is most often grown in pots as a houseplant and should be treated like cactus—grown in a sandy, well-drained soil and watered only when the soil surface feels dry.

Propagation is from offsets—baby plants that appear around the base of the mother plant. In areas that are completely frost-free, aloe plants will survive outdoors. It is a popular choice for dry landscape gardens.

The tips of the plant are broken off and the inside gel rubbed onto skin for the relief of burns, especially sunburn. The gel can be spooned out of the leaves and used as a natural skin conditioner.

Mints

(Mentha species and hybrids)

The family of mints is large and easily identified by its characteristic square stems. The leaves vary according to variety, but most are spear-shaped and serrated. The two most common mints are *M. spicata* (spearmint) and *M.* × *piperita* (peppermint), both hardy perennials. They look similar, though peppermint has darker, shinier foliage and pink rather than white flower spikes, while spearmint has more rounded leaves. Mint plants grow to 3 feet (90cm) tall and spread aggressively from stoloniferous roots.

Propagate by division and by root cuttings, since any section of root with a stem node will produce new feeder roots in moist soil. Mint plants prefer full sun and a humus-rich, moisture-retentive soil. To prevent mints from escaping into other areas of the garden, consider growing them in sunken sections of a chimney flue. If not contained, mints can be invasive and may represent a nuisance in the garden. Space plants at least 3 feet (90cm) apart.

The primary culinary use for mint is as a garnish for lamb, for which it is chopped fine and mixed with vinegar. This sauce also goes well with boiled potatoes and peas. Mints make a refreshing tea. Not only is the flavor invigorating, the vapors of a hot brewed tea help to clear the sinuses. Since the family of mints is so varied, and the aromas so diverse, it's worth creating a special mint garden (see page 49).

Many mints have attractive variegated leaves. This variety, known as golden mint, is pleasantly apple-scented.

Nasturtium

(*Tropaeolum majus*)

Dwarf nasturtiums, like this 'Whirlibird' cultivar, can be tucked in a corner of the garden to provide a dab of brilliant color. Nasturtiums have long been a treasured ornamental, and can be trained to clamber over a fence or up a trellis or to trail attractively from a hanging basket. Both the leaves and flowers are edible, and look lovely in salads and gourmet sandwiches.

Nasturtium flowers resemble pansies in that they have fairly flat faces, but grow in a brighter color range that includes bright orange, scarlet red, crimson, bright pink, and apricot. The dark or bright green leaves are shaped like parasols, and all parts of the plant—including the seeds, leaves, stems, and flowers—are edible as a peppery-flavored garnish.

There are both vining kinds of nasturtiums and dwarf, compact varieties. Some have flowers with spurs, which makes them grow sideways on the plant, while others—like 'Whirlibird'—are spurless, allowing the flowers to face up and present a more colorful display when grown for ornamental value.

Nasturtiums are tender annuals with large, pea-size, white seeds which can be sown 1 inch (2.5cm) deep directly into the garden after frost danger, or started early indoors 6 weeks before outdoor planting. The plants bloom best in full sun, when the nights are still cool. They also demand good drainage. If the soil is too fertile, it stimulates more foliage growth than flowers. The dwarf varieties are excellent for growing in containers, including window boxes and hanging baskets.

The soft parts of the plant can be chopped fine to add a piquancy to salads; the edible flowers are especially useful since their cheerful faces and bright colors are greatly appealing. The hard seeds are edible when pickled. Nasturtiums are highly attractive to hummingbirds.

Oreganos

(O r i g a n u m   v u l g a r e
a n d   o t h e r   s p e c i e s
a n d   h y b r i d s)

There are many varieties of oregano, some tall and others low-growing. The cultivar 'Aurea', shown here, makes a splendid groundcover. A favorite ingredient of Italian cooking, oregano is often used in combination with basil and marjoram, to which it is closely related.

riganum vulgare is the traditional oregano used in herb gardens because of its hardiness, attractive purple flower clusters, and smooth, spear-shaped leaves. But its flavor is not as intense as sweet marjoram or some of the more tender hybrid oreganos, such as *O. × marjoricum* (commonly called Italian oregano). There are also some beautiful oreganos of landscape value, such as *O. vulgare* 'Aureum', a low-spreading plant with small, buttonlike leaves that makes a beautiful edging or container plant. Unfortunately, it is only moderately hardy and will rarely survive north of Zone 7 because it will not live through the cold winters.

The hybrid oreganos are usually sterile and therefore must be grown from division. However, the common *O. vulgare* is easily grown from seed, started indoors 6 weeks before outdoor planting. Sow the seeds just below the soil surface, and transplant resulting seedlings into the garden after danger of severe frost has passed. Plants prefer full sun and good drainage, but tolerate impoverished soil. Space plants at least 2 feet (60cm) apart.

Orris

(Iris germanica var. florentina)

Orris is the root of a hardy perennial iris that resembles the common ornamental bearded iris. It has sword-shaped, blue-green leaves and white or pale blue iris flowers in late spring. It grows 2 feet (60cm) tall. The roots are swollen, horizontal, and knobbly, lying close to the surface, usually with their tops exposed to the sun. The root has a pleasant, sweet fragrance, and cut into small lumps it is valuable as a potpourri fixative. Since some people are allergic to orris, a useful alternative is sweet flag root (*Acorus calamus*), which is similar in appearance to orris, but instead of an irislike flower it has an inconspicuous powdery plume. Unlike orris, sweet flag will tolerate boggy soil.

Orris is propagated by dividing the rhizomes. Any section of rhizome with a crown of leaves will root and form a new plant, but wait until after it flowers. When planting the rhizome, do not completely cover it with soil. Position it in the soil like a boat, with ⅔ of the root submerged and ⅓ exposed to the sun. It demands a sunny position and good drainage. Space plants at least 12 inches (30cm) apart to give their roots room to grow.

The root, either chopped into small cubes or sliced into shavings, is an important ingredient in potpourri since it is itself sweetly fragrant and absorbs adjacent oils, allowing potpourri mixtures to last longer.

The pale blue flowers of orris closely resemble those of bearded irises, of which orris is a variety. Most commonly used as a fixative in potpourris, orris is also supremely ornamental.

Parsley

(*Petroselinum crispum*)

Plain-leaf parsley is considered the most flavorful, but the curly-leaf type is more decorative. You might consider growing both types to get the best of both worlds.

Parsley is a hardy biennial that is best grown as a hardy annual. It grows compact, 12-inch (30cm) -high mounds of leaves the first year, followed by coarse, erect flower stems with small white flowers the second season. After it flowers, the plant goes to seed and falls apart. There are both plain-leaf and curly-leaf parsleys; there is also a plain-leaf kind, called 'Hamburg', which produces an edible root that is shaped like a large carrot.

Seed germination can be erratic unless a stable 70°F (21°C) soil temperature can be maintained. Fast seed starting is assured if the seed is placed in a moist paper napkin and held at room temperature for a week. All sprouted or swollen seeds can then be transferred directly to the garden, and covered with ¼ inch (0.5cm) of fine soil. Parsley prefers full sun and good drainage.

The parsley worm can attack the plant, but it does not do a lot of damage. (The worm eventually turns into a beautiful swallow-tail butterfly.) However, deer and groundhogs love parsley, and where these are a problem, consider covering a row of plants with a mound of chicken wire for protection.

Parsley is especially good to use finely chopped as a garnish for fish, egg dishes, soups, herbal sauces, and potatoes. Sprigs of parsley are used as a decorative garnish on buffet tables. Parsley is an excellent candidate for container growing, holding its flavor even through winter months. Parsley is also beautiful mixed with flowers in window boxes, and used as an edging to flower borders.

Rosemary

(Rosmarinus officinalis)

This gorgeous weeping form of rosemary, called 'Prostratus', produces an abundant cascade of blue flowers, but, like other rosemaries, needs a mild climate to over-winter outdoors.

Rosemary is a somewhat tender woody shrub with evergreen, needlelike, aromatic leaves and small pale blue flowers that appear in summer. The plants grow to 4 feet (1.2m) tall, and though the common habit is upright and bushy, there are prostrate and weeping forms that have value as landscape plants in areas with mild winters (Zone 7 and south).

Since seed germination is erratic and growth slow, propagation is most successful from tip cuttings. These plants prefer a sunny position, acid soil, and good drainage. They do not like the high humidity and hot summers of the deep south. In northern gardens, rosemary is best grown in a pot (minimum 1 gallon [3.7L] capacity) so it may be taken indoors in areas with freezing winter temperatures. Trimming and pruning can produce some interesting topiary shapes.

Rosemary is popular as a garnish for poultry and meats, especially sausage and stuffing. But its flavor is strong, so use it sparingly. In areas with mild winters, rosemary plants make excellent low hedges.

Rue

(*Ruta graveolens*)

Rue is a hardy bushy perennial that grows to 2 feet (60cm) tall, with attractive, pungent, blue-green cloverlike leaves and clusters of yellow flowers that bloom in summer.

It is usually propagated from seed, although the most beautiful ornamental forms with the deepest blue coloration, such as 'Blue Beauty' and the dwarf 'Blue Mound', must be propagated from division. Start seed indoors 8 weeks before outdoor planting. Cover the seeds with just enough soil to anchor them and transplant seedlings into the garden after danger of frost has passed. Rue prefers full sun and good drainage. Space the plants at least 2 feet (60cm) apart.

At one time, all kinds of supernatural properties were attributed to rue, but modern research has suggested caution in using rue in any form except ornamental, and as a decorative component of herbal wreaths. Handling the stems without gloves can give some people a skin rash.

Above: 'Blue Mound' rue is loaded with yellow blooms. Below: Saffron can be planted to grow through turf.

Saffron

(*Crocus sativus*)

The finest saffron grows in Spain and Kashmir. It is by far the world's costliest spice. A type of autumn-blooming crocus, plants are grown from bulbs, which produce spiky green leaves in summer and flowers on bare stems in the autumn. At the center of each cup-shaped bloom is a pair of long reddish filaments. These are removed by tweezers and dried in batches on screens to make a bitter flavoring valued in certain gourmet dishes. The filaments are also the source of a deep yellow dye.

Saffron crocus prefers areas with long summers. The bulbs are usually available from mail-order sources in the autumn, but in northern gardens (Zone 7 and above), there is insufficient time for the plant to grow a clump of leaves, and then to flower. Therefore, it is best to first plant the bulbs in a container, and allow the plant to set leaves and flower indoors in a sunny window. Space at least 2 inches (5cm) apart. In spring the bulbs can then be set outside in the garden in a sunny, well-drained position to grow leaves in summer and flower in autumn.

The dried filaments are crumbled into rice dishes, such as Spanish paella and many Asian and Mediterranean dishes. Store the herb by placing the dried filaments in a plastic bag and keeping it refrigerated. Because saffron is so difficult to grow in quantity and so costly to buy, it is possible to use orange marigold petals as a substitute (see pages 94-95).

The variegated forms of sage are indispensable when creating a tapestry effect with foliage. In addition to green-and-white forms, there are sages in shades of purple, gold, and pink.

Sage
(*Salvia officinalis*)

Like mints and scented-leaf geraniums, sage is a large plant family. Many sages are useful in herb gardens, some grown to use as a garnish, others grown purely for ornamental effect and fragrance. Common sage is a clump-forming hardy perennial with woody stems and decorative, gray-green, lance-shaped leaves that appear to be blistered. The leaves have a strong, camphorlike flavor. In early summer, the plants produce spires of decorative blue flowers. Common sage has several interesting variegated forms, including golden, purple, and tricolored. Other species have foliage with a fruity scent, such as *S. pomifera* (apple), *S. elegans* (pineapple), and *S. dorisiana* (grapefruit).

Propagate sage from stem cuttings and division. Although it is a perennial, plants rarely live beyond a third season, when they become brittle and fall apart. They prefer full sun and a well-drained soil. Space plants at least 12 inches (30cm) apart. The variegated forms are especially good to group together in containers.

Sage is a popular seasoning for poultry stuffing, sausage, stews, herbal sauces, hams, and fish. Store leaves dried in screw-top jars.

Savory

(S a t u r e j a   m o n t a n a ,
S .   h o r t e n s i s)

'Repens' winter savory is a dwarf, mounded form that is more decorative than any of the summer savories.

Although there are two kinds of savory grown in herb gardens (winter savory and summer savory), it is the summer savory that is the most pungent and useful as a seasoning. Unfortunately, it is not a very attractive plant, growing loose, upright stems up to 3 feet (90cm) tall, with slender leaves. Winter savory, especially the dwarf form, 'Repens', is more ornamental in appearance. It forms an attractive cushion just 6 inches (15cm) tall and is covered with masses of white flowers in late summer. Both winter and summer savory are hardy perennials.

Propagate savory either by seed, division, or cuttings. Seed should be started indoors 8 weeks before outdoor planting. Cover seed with just a thin layer of soil and transplant seedlings into the garden after danger of frost has passed. Plant savory in full sun into a well-drained soil , spacing the plants at least 12 inches (30cm) apart.

This herb is mostly used as a seasoning for bean dishes. It also adds an interesting flavor to soups, stews, and potato dishes. The dried leaves may be stored by hanging in bunches. The variety 'Repens' makes a good pot plant, although its aromatic properties are slight.

Sorrel

(*Rumex acetosa*)

Care should be taken to prevent sorrel from seeding into garden soil, as it can become a persistent weed. Instead, plant it in pots or in small beds with sharply defined borders of concrete or another man-made edging.

This hardy perennial grows a clump of long, broad, wavy leaves that can be harvested as an edible green for most of the year, even during winter months. In mid-summer, the plants produce clusters of reddish flowers, which are followed by brown flaky seeds that persist on the stems a long time.

Sorrel is best propagated by division. The plants also grow easily from seeds sown directly into the garden several weeks before the last frost date in spring, or in late summer and early autumn. Sow seed ¼ inch (0.5cm) deep, spaced 8 to 12 inches (20 to 30cm) apart. Sorrel likes a sunny position, but will tolerate light shade. It is not fussy about soil provided drainage is good. Unless you want the flower stalks for dried arrangements and self-seeding, prune them off to keep the plants bushy.

Sorrel leaves have a tender, bittersweet flavor and are good added to soups and salads, and for stuffing with ground meat, cabbage, or cheese, like grape leaves. Use only the youngest leaves.

Sweet Annie

(A r t e m i s i a   a n n u a)

A tall, feathery, fast-growing annual, sweet Annie has no culinary value, but it has a wonderful, sweet aroma similar to eucalyptus, with powerful deodorizing qualities. Growing to 5 feet (1.5m) tall, it produces masses of inconspicuous, small yellow flowers in late summer.

Sweet Annie is easily grown from seeds direct-sown into the garden, covered with just enough soil to anchor them. In fact, the plants will self-seed readily, so that in subsequent years you can propagate from volunteers that will spring up all around the old plant. Space plants at least 2 feet (60cm) apart.

The long, tall stems are cut from the base and bunched for drying upside down. They are then used mostly in dried herbal wreaths, as a deodorant to mask unpleasant household odors, and as an ingredient in potpourri. Simply snap off a dried section of stem with leaves or seed pods, crush it into a powder and sprinkle on the floor to fill a room with its pleasant, spicy aroma.

Sweet Cicely

(*Myrrhis odorata*)

A hardy perennial, sweet Cicely grows heavily indented, aromatic leaves and clusters of white flowers in early summer. The plants grow to 3 feet (90cm) high and self-sow readily.

This herb is usually grown from seed sown ¼ inch (0.5cm) deep directly into the garden several weeks before the last frost date or in late summer and early autumn, since the freshest seed ensures the highest rate of germination. Grow in full sun and well-drained soil.

The anise-scented leaves are chopped and used as a seasoning for fresh fruit salads, green salads, and meat dishes. The dried leaves are also added to potpourri.

In late summer, sweet Cicely displays dramatic rounded flower umbels on branching stalks. The flowers are followed by large brown seeds.

Tarragon

(*Artemisia dracunculus*)

There are two kinds of tarragon: French tarragon, the preferred kind because of its aniselike aromatic qualities, and Russian tarragon, a less desirable plant because of its poor aromatic qualities. French tarragon is sterile, does not set seed, and can be propagated only by division or cuttings; Russian tarragon will grow easily from seed. Both are hardy perennials and

grow to 3 feet (90cm) tall, forming clumps of slender stems with narrow, smooth leaves. Tarragon rarely flowers, and when it does the flowers are green and so tiny as to be inconspicuous.

The French variety of tarragon is called 'Sativa', and is the only kind worth growing. Give the plants full sun and soil with good drainage. Space plants at least 2 feet (60cm) apart.

Tarragon is used as a seasoning in salads, soups, and herbal sauces, as well as with fish and poultry. It makes a tasty vinegar, and may be dried for later use.

Be careful when buying tarragon, as many varieties sold in nurseries are the flavorless Russian tarragon rather than the French tarragon prized for its sharp, anise taste and aroma.

Thyme, English

(*Thymus vulgaris*)

There are many varieties of thyme, with varying degrees of aromatic content. Some of those popular in herb gardens are quite tall and bushy; others are low and spreading. Leaf color can vary from dark green to yellow and silver. The masses of tubular flowers that usually occur in summer can range from white through many shades of pink to purple. English thyme is the plant most associated with herb gardens. It adds a spicy flavor to most meat dishes, including poultry and beef. English thyme grows to 2 feet (60cm) tall, and is covered in slender, short, evergreen leaves that resemble pine needles.

Thyme is a hardy perennial that is most easily propagated by division. Plants like full sun, but tolerate poor soil, provided drainage is good. They will grow contentedly

Most varieties of thyme bloom in early summer. These spreading, ground-hugging plants are particularly useful herbs for edging paths.

on dry walls and between flagstones. Use the low-spreading kinds as an edging along paths and plant them among cracks in paving. The most beautiful effect I ever saw was an entire lawn area composed of low-growing varieties of thyme in a patchwork quilt of different leaf colors and flower colors. To create such a colorful carpet, space plants no more than 6 inches (15cm) apart, so that they can knit together by the end of one season.

The leaves are used sparingly as a flavor enhancer for poultry stuffing; thyme is also sprinkled into meat sauces, stews, and soups. Lemon thyme (*Thymus citriodorus*) has a pleasant citrus aroma and mosquito-repellent properties when rubbed on exposed skin. The leaves may be dried for use at a later date. Simply gather a bunch of stems together and air-dry upside down.

Watercress

(*Nasturtium officinale*)

This hardy perennial produces rosettes of succulent, heart-shaped, glossy green, vitamin-rich leaves and clusters of tiny white flowers. During winter and cool spring and autumn months the rosettes stay tight and low to the ground, but in hot weather they elongate and go to seed. However, there is barely a day of the year that you cannot harvest fresh watercress as an edible salad green.

Contrary to popular belief, watercress does not need water in which to grow. Although it thrives in shallow running streams, with its roots permanently covered in water, watercress will grow in any humus-rich loam soil, mulched to retain moisture. Native to Europe, watercress is naturalized all across North America. Though watercress is easily grown from seed, direct-sown into the garden during cool weather and lightly covered with soil, it is most easily propagated by dividing up an existing clump and transplanting it to a sunny location. If you do plant watercress in a stream, make sure that each transplant is rooted in gravel (or mud) and anchor the root with a stone to stop it from being washed away. Watercress also grows well in pots, especially if the base of the pot rests in water.

Watercress is a wonderful all-season substitute for spinach. Use it alone as the basis for a delicious salad, or mix the leaves with other salad greens. A handful of watercress can be chopped fine and added, with onions, to a bland potato soup to make a delicious, green-colored, flavorful watercress soup. It can also be served as a cooked side dish, just like spinach.

I can honestly say that if I could have only one herb in my garden it would be watercress. It is such a thrill to be able to walk down to my stream and pick it fresh any day of the year, even with snow on the ground. When sections of the stream are frozen, I break the ice and find the watercress alive and well underneath in the crystal clear water. Other kinds of cress (such as curly cress) are a favorite ingredient in egg sandwiches, but small sprigs of watercress can be substituted.

Watercress creates a dense weave of leaves when grown in water, persisting all through the winter months.

Woodruff

(*Galium odoratum*)

Woodruff likes to be planted under the shade of trees. It has a rapid, spreading habit, ideal for covering vast expanses of woodland.

Woodruff is a low-spreading, shade-loving hardy perennial with delicate, attractive, star-shaped leaves and clusters of small white flowers that appear in early summer. It grows to just 6 inches (15cm) tall.

Woodruff is most easily propagated by division of the aggressive roots. Although seed is also available, germination is erratic. These plants prefer a shady location and a humus-rich, moist soil. Space plants at least 12 inches (30cm) apart to create a beautiful, fragrant groundcover.

The leaves are mostly used as an infusion to flavor May wine, but the pleasant aroma can also be appreciated as a refreshing tea. This herb is ideal for creating a weed-suffocating carpet under trees and along woodland paths.

Wormwoods
(*Artemisia* species)

There are numerous species and hybrids of wormwood that at one time were used to make medicines and flavor alcoholic drinks, but be warned that they are now all considered dangerous to ingest. Common wormwood (*Artemisia absinthium*)—the sources of the liqueur called absinthe—is regarded as an addictive substance, and can result in seizures and even death. In spite of this, various wormwoods are valued for their silvery foliage, not only to create beautiful dried herbal wreaths and shimmering accents in the garden, but also for use as natural insect repellents. Common wormwood and its close relative southernwood (*A. abrotanum*) are particularly admired, and grow to 4 feet (1.2m) tall.

Southernwood, especially the cultivar 'Tangerine', named for its appealing citrusy scent, is the species most often seen in herb gardens, though several others are popular, largely for their ornamental contributions. These include *A. schmidtiana* 'Silver Mound', which grows to 18 inches (45.5 cm); 'Silver Brocade' beach wormwood (*A. stellerana* 'Silver Brocade'), which grows to 18 inches (45.5cm); 'Silver King' white sage (*A. ludoviciana* 'Silver King'), which reaches a height of 3 feet (90cm); and a hybrid 'Powis Castle', which grows into a wide spreading shrub that often reaches 4 feet (1.2m) in height.

Most of the ornamental wormwoods are grown from divisions and cuttings, but southernwood may also be propagated from seeds. Cover the seeds with just enough soil to anchor them and space them at least 3 feet (90cm) apart. Water artemisia species sparingly. Like most silver-foliaged plants, they come from dry areas and the roots are susceptible to rot in poorly drained soils. Flowers are usually small, creamy white, and inconspicuous. Cut back established plants heavily before new growth in spring to maintain a tidy appearance.

The lacelike foliage of many species of wormwoods is a natural insect repellent.

About
the
Author

Derek Fell is a writer and photographer who specializes in gardening, with an emphasis on step-by-step gardening concepts and garden design. He lives in Bucks County, Pennsylvania, at historic Cedaridge Farm, Tinicum Township, where he cultivates extensive award-winning flower and vegetable gardens that have been featured in *Architectural Digest, Garden Design, Beautiful Gardens, Gardens Illustrated, American Nurseryman,* and *Mid-Atlantic Country* magazines. Born and educated in England, he first worked for seven years with Europe's largest seed company, then moved to Pennsylvania in 1964 to work for Burpee Seeds as their catalog manager, a position he held for six years before taking on duties as executive director of the All-America Selections (the national seed trials) and the National Garden Bureau (an information office sponsored by the American seed industry). Now the author of more than fifty garden books and calendars, he has traveled widely throughout North America, also documenting gardens in Europe, Africa, South America, New Zealand, and Asia. His most recent books are *Renoir's Garden* (Simon & Schuster), *The Impressionist Garden* (Crown), *500 Perennial Garden Ideas* (Simon & Schuster), and *Glorious Flowers* (Friedman/Fairfax), co-authored with his wife, Carolyn.

A frequent contributor to *Architectural Digest* and *Woman's Day* magazines, Derek Fell is the winner of more awards from the Garden Writers Association of America than any other garden writer. He also worked as a consultant on gardening to the White House during the Ford Administration.

Wall calendars, greeting cards, and art posters featuring Derek Fell's photography are published worldwide. He has lectured on photography and the gardens of the great Impressionist painters at numerous art museums, including the Smithsonian Institution in Washington, D.C.; the Philadelphia Museum of Art; the Barnes Foundation, Philadelphia; and the Denver Art Museum, Colorado. He is also host of a regular garden show for the QVC cable television shopping channel, entitled *Step-by-Step Gardening,* which is plugged into fifty million homes.

Fell's highly acclaimed *Step-by-Step Gardening* mail-order perennial plant catalogs for Spring Hill Nurseries (North America's largest mail-order nursery) reach an audience of home gardeners estimated to be more than three million in spring and autumn. He is a former president of the Hobby Greenhouse Association, a former director of the Garden Writers Association of America, the president of the International Test Gardeners Association, and a cofounder of the American Gardening Association.

A complete list of published works follows.

Books by Derek Fell

(Asterisk indicates co-authorship.)

The White House Vegetable Garden. 1976, Exposition.

House Plants for Fun & Profit. 1978, Bookworm.

How to Photograph Flowers, Plants, & Landscapes. 1980, HP Books.

Vegetables: How to Select, Grow, and Enjoy. 1982, HP Books.

Annuals: How to Select, Grow, and Enjoy. 1983, HP Books.

Deerfield: An American Garden Through Four Seasons. 1986, Pidcock Press.

Trees & Shrubs. 1986, HP Books.

Garden Accents. 1987, Henry Holt (Inspired Garden in the United Kingdom).

*Discover Anguilla. 1988, Caribbean Concepts.

*Home Landscaping. 1988, Simon & Schuster.

The One-Minute Gardener. 1988, Running Press.

A Kid's First Gardening Book. 1989, Running Press.

*Three Year Garden Journal. 1989, Starwood.

*Ornamental Grass Gardening. 1989, HP Books.

*The Complete Garden Planning Manual. 1989, HP Books.

The Essential Gardener. 1990, Crown.

Essential Roses. 1990, Crown.

Essential Annuals. 1990, Crown.

Essential Bulbs. 1990, Crown.

Essential Herbs. 1990, Crown.

Essential Perennials. 1990, Crown.

Essential Shrubs. 1990, Crown.

The Easiest Flower to Grow. 1990, Ortho.

*550 Home Landscaping Ideas. 1991, Simon & Schuster.

Renoir's Garden. 1991, Simon & Schuster.

Beautiful Bucks County. 1991, Cedaridge.

* The Encyclopedia of Ornamental Grasses. 1992, Smithmark.

The Encyclopedia of Flowers. 1993, Smithmark.

*550 Perennial Garden Ideas. 1993, Simon & Schuster.

The Impressionist Garden. 1994, Crown.

The Pennsylvania Gardener. 1995, Camino Books.

*Practical Gardening. 1995, Friedman/Fairfax.

*Gardens of Philadelphia & the Delaware Valley. 1995, Temple University Press.

Perennial Gardening with Derek Fell. 1996, Friedman/Fairfax.

Vegetable Gardening with Derek Fell. 1996, Friedman/Fairfax.

Derek Fell's Handy Garden Guides: Annuals. 1996, Friedman/Fairfax.

Derek Fell's Handy Garden Guides: Bulbs. 1996, Friedman/Fairfax.

Derek Fell's Handy Garden Guides: Perennials. 1996, Friedman/Fairfax.

Derek Fell's Handy Garden Guides: Roses. 1996, Friedman/Fairfax.

Glorious Flowers. 1996, Friedman/Fairfax.

Bulb Gardening with Derek Fell. 1997, Friedman/Fairfax.

Calendars

Great Gardens (Portal)

The Impressionist Garden (Portal)

The Gardening Year (Portal)

Perennials (Starwood)

Flowering Shrubs (Starwood)

Flowering Bulbs (Starwood)

Northeast Gardens Calendar (Starwood)

Mid-Atlantic Gardens Calendar (Starwood)

Southern Gardens Calendar (Starwood)

California Gardens Calendar (Starwood)

Pacific Northwest Gardens Calendar (Starwood)

Art Posters

Deerfield Garden (Portal)

Spring Garden (Portal)

Monet's Bridge (Portal)

Mail Order Sources

for Seeds and Plants

*New England
and
Mid-Atlantic*

Cricket Hill Herb Farm,
Ltd.
Glen Street
Rowley, MA 01969

Fox Hollow Herbs
P.O. Box 148
McGrann, PA 16236

Catalog $1, non-refundable

Glade Valley Nursery
9226 Links Road
Walkersville, MD 21793

*Herbs and scented geraniums.
No charge for price list*

Hartman's Herb Farm
1026 Old Dana Road
Barre, MA 01005

*Catalog $2, refunded with first
order*

The Herb Barn
H.C. 64, Box 435D
Trout Run, PA 17771

Send $.50 or SASE for price list

Kingfisher, Inc.
   Halycon Garden
   Products
P.O. Box 75
Wexford, PA 15090

*Catalog and guide to growing
herbs $2, non-refundable*

Logee's Greenhouses
141 North Street
Danielson, CT 06239

*Catalog $3, refunded with first
order*

Maryland's Herb Basket
Box 131
Millington, MD 21651

Catalog $1, non-refundable

The Rosemary House
120 South Market Street
Mechanicsburg, PA 17055

Catalog $3, non-refundable

Tinmouth Channel Farm
RR 1, Box 428B
Tinmouth, VT 05773

Catalog $2, non-refundable

Triple Oaks Nursery
Route 47
Franklinville, NJ 08322

Send SASE for free price list

Well-Sweep Herb Farm
317 Mt. Bethel Road
Port Murray, NJ 07865

Catalog $2, non-refundable

*South and
Southeast*

Bo's Nursery
12743 Gillard Road
Winter Garden, FL 34787

Send SASE for free price list

Good Hollow Greenhouse
   & Herbarium
50 Slate Rock Mill Road
Taft, TN 38488

Send SASE for free price list

McCrory's Sunny Hill
   Herb Farm
35152 LaPlace Court
Eustis, FL 32726

*Price list $.50, refunded with
first order*

Rasland Farm
NC 82 at US 13
Godwin, NC 28344-9712

Catalog $3, non-refundable

Rose Hill Herbs &
   Perennials
Rt. 4, Box 377
Amherst, VA 24521

Catalog $2

Sandy Mush Herb
   Nursery
Rt. 2, Surrett Cove Road
Leicester, NC 28748

*Catalog and handbook $4, non-
refundable*

Southern Seeds
P.O. Box 2091
Melbourne, FL 32902

Catalog $1, non-refundable

Village Arbors
1804 Saugahatchee Road
Auburn, AL 36830

Catalog $1

Midwest

Alyce's Herbs
P.O. Box 9563
Madison, WI 53715

Catalog $1

Companion Plants
7247 North Coolville
Ridge Road
Athens, OH 45701

Catalog $2, non-refundable

The Farmhouse
10,000 N.W. 70th Street
Grimes, IA 50111

Catalog $1, non-refundable

Fox Hill Farm
Box 7
Parma, MI 49269

Catalog $1

The Gathered Herb &
Greenhouse
12114 N. State Road
Otisville, MI 48463

*Catalog $2, refunded with first
order*

The Herb Barn
1955 Greenley Avenue
Benton Harbor, MI
49022

*Seeds only. Catalog $1, refunded
with first order*

Herbs-Liscious
1702 South 6th Street
Marshalltown, IA 50158

Lily of the Valley Herb
Farm
3969 Fox Avenue
Minerva, OH 44657

*Plant price list $1, product price
list $1, refunded with first orders*

Shady Hill Gardens
831 Walnut Street
Batavia, IL 60510

*Scented geraniums. Catalog $2,
refunded with first order.*

*Great Plains
and Rocky
Mountain States*

The Gourmet Gardener
4000 West 126th Street
Leawood, KS 66209

Catalog $2

Rabbit Shadow Farm
2880n East Highway 402
Loveland, CO 80537

Catalog $1, non-refundable

*Texas and
Southwest*

Hilltop Herb Farm at
Chain O'Lakes Resort
P.O. Box 325
Romayor, TX 77368

Send SASE for free price list

California

Heirloom Garden Seeds
P.O. Box 138
Guerneville, CA 95446

Catalog $3

Sheperd's Garden Seeds
6116 Highway 9
Felton, CA 95018

Catalog $1, non-refundable

Taylor's Herb Gardens
1535 Lone Oak Road
Vista, CA 92084

Catalog $3, non-refundable

Northwest

Dutch Mill Herb Farm
Rt. 2, Box 190
Forest Grove, OR 97116

*Lavender specialist. Send SASE
for free price list*

Goodwin Creek Gardens
P.O. Box 83
Williams, OR 97544

Catalog $1, non-refundable

Nichols Garden Nursery
1190 N. Pacific Highway
Albany, OR 97321

Catalog $1

Canada

Dacha Barinka
25232 Strathcona Road
Chilliwack, British
Columbia
Canada V2P 3AT2

*Catalog $1, refunded with first
order*

Rawlinson Garden Seed
269 College Road
Truro, Nova Scotia
Canada B2N 2P6

*Catalog free within Canada; $1
to U.S. customers, refunded with
first $10 order*

Richters
357 Highway 47
Goodwood, Ontario
Canada LOC 1AO

Seed and plant catalog $2

Tregunno Seeds
c/o Ontario Seed CO.,
Ltd.
P.O. Box 144, 16 King
Street South
Waterloo, Ontario
Canada N2J 3Z9

Catalog free

Other Sources

Herb Societies

The Herb Society of America
9019 Kirtland-Chardon Road
Mentor, OH 44060

International Herb Growers and
Marketers Association
Box 281
Silver Spring, PA 62814

Books

Johnson, Marsha Peter. *Gourmet Vinegars: How to Make and Cook with Them.* Lake Oswego, OR: Culinary Arts Ltd., 1989.

Krachmal, Connie and Arnold. *Complete Illustrated Book of Dyes from Natural Sources.* New York: Doubleday, 1974.

Simmons, Adelma G. *Country Wreaths from Caprilands.* Emmaus, PA: Rodale Press, 1989.

Webb, David W. *Making Potpourri, Colognes and Soaps.* Blueridge Summit, PA: Tab Books, 1988.

Woodring Smith, Leona. *Forgotten Art of Flower Cookery, The.* Gretna, LA: Pelican, 1973, 1985, 1990.

Index